Cocktail
Nation

Cocktail

Cosmic Cocktails, Space-Age Shots,

and Other Rituals of Release

Nation

for the Jaded and Refined

Beverly West and Kim Doi

BERKLEY BOOKS, NEW YORK

This book is an original publication of
The Berkley Publishing Group.

COCKTAIL NATION

A Berkley Book / published by
arrangement with the authors

PRINTING HISTORY
Berkley trade paperback edition / August 1997

The Putnam Berkley World Wide Web site address is
http://www.berkley.com

ISBN: 0-425-15852-7

BERKLEY®
Berkley Books are published by The Berkley Publishing Group,
200 Madison Avenue, New York, New York 10016.
BERKLEY and the "B" design
are trademarks belonging to Berkley Publishing Corporation.

PRINTED IN THE UNITED STATES OF AMERICA

10   9   8   7   6   5   4   3   2   1

Dedication

To everyone who drove us to drink

Acknowledgments

Thanks to all our friends at Berkley: Denise Silvestro, Bill Rue, Sandy Su, and especially our editor, Barry Neville, for his vision, enthusiasm, and exhaustively researched grasp of lounge culture.

Thanks also to John "Cardinal Puff" Giuliano, Nancy Peske, Ron Hayden, Danny "The Baton-Twirling Bartender" Heckman, and of course, Sean McKenna, whose door, like Denny's, was always open.

And as always, thanks to our agent, Kevin "Hepcat" McShane, for laying down the bass line and keeping the beat.

Contents

Introduction   xi

1 The Well-Stocked Bar   1

2 Straight Shooters   5

3 Staken Not Shirred—The Neo-Martini   50

4 Retro Cocktails—Rococo Recipes from
Days of Yore   91

5 Mellow Jell-O Shots   116

6 Nonalcoholic Drinks   123

7 There's Got to Be a Morning After—
Surefire Hangover Remedies   124

8 The Last Word in Good Taste—Tiny
Tempters to Spread Your Reputation as
a Knowing Host or Hostess   132

9 Gay and Amusing Party Ideas   138

Important Phone Numbers   142

Favorite Drinks, Mine and My Friends'   143

Really Disgusting Drinks That I'll Never Drink Again Myself but May Consider Serving My Friends   144

Audience Participation Page   145

Index of Drinks   146

Introduction

Greetings, friends! Welcome to the urbane and elegant world of the cosmopolite. Here, life is a lounge, and the atmosphere is pregnant with the seductive recklessness of a bygone era. Close your eyes and you can imagine dashing men in narrow lapels and slinky dames in strapless numbers cut on the bias, sipping expertly chilled martinis and single malts, neat. Feel the zu, zu, zu, of the sibilant samba, and imagine yourself dancing the mambo over the precipice of total economic and cultural collapse, wearing cat-eye glasses and a lampshade on your head. This is the way of the swinger.

The lesson imparted by the bon vivants of yesteryear and their tosspot tenacity is that nothing is so dire that it cannot be solved by a few shakers of cosmopolitans and a bowl of bar snacks. You say the corporatization of Hollywood has put the brakes on your career as an avant-garde filmmaker? It doesn't matter. You've discovered that your advanced degree in twentieth-century polemics only qualifies you to copy, collate, or steam milk for minimum wage? Pish posh. You insist that your inner realm is unfurnished, and despite the many amazing advances in interactive software, you still can't initialize your modem? *Ça fait rien*.

The ritual of release takes the sting out of all these contemporary calamities. As a citizen of the cocktail nation, you will linger in a polished hemisphere, where the repartee is witty and crisp and your future is bright. After your second drink, you've forgotten all about that pesky student loan, and the free Buffalo wings have become edible. By your fourth, you and the fuzzled inebriate next to you have figured out how to accomplish world peace and ordered another round to celebrate your Nobel Prize.

And if after all this, you're still feeling a little blue . . . there's always the shot girl at Señor Frog's.

One

The Well-Stocked Bar

Every civilized gin palace must contain the following essentials:

Glassware

The variety of available glassware has proliferated throughout the course of mixological history to the extent that it is now possible to earn an advanced degree in twentieth-century glassware as it relates to a theory of pure libation in the postatomic age. For our undergraduate purposes, however, it is only necessary that you find something that, unlike that boozy Bacchanalian who passed out in your bathroom at the last toga party, can hold its liquor. The recipes in this book will call for shot glasses. There are two varieties of shot glasses: small-mouth, and large-mouth. You can tell the difference between them by putting the shot glass in your mouth and seeing how far your lips stretch. If your mouth is making a little O like Cindy Lou Hoo, that's a small-mouth glass. You will also need martini glasses, cocktail glasses (which look like martini glasses only narrower and deeper), and a cocktail shaker. All of these receptacles can be found in any housewares store. Of course, if you want to save money, you can always pinch equipment from your dad's bar or substitute with whatever you've got handy: flower vases, old pasta sauce jars, Poland Spring bottles, bath tubs, or your science geek roommate's aquarium (of course, you'll need a straw for these last two).

Ice

Preferably the frozen variety, and please, square cubes only. There is something aesthetically offensive about a piece of ice in the shape of a naked woman's torso or a frigid football polluting the pristine confluence of a perfectly executed potation. Ice is a hard-edge medium.

Alcohol

Stock up on a watershed of the most hellacious hooch you can lay your hands on.

Mixers and Garnishes

By way of mixers, it's wise to stock a generous supply of anything that will cut the taste. Garnishes are a bit more complicated. The most commonly used garnishes for the drinks in this book are made from fruit. A lime squeeze is created by cutting a lime into quarters. One lime quarter is squeezed into the drink and then thrown into the glass. A twist is a small section of the lemon rind, best made with a twist maker, which can be found in most liquor, grocery, or housewares stores. We don't recommend that amateur bartenders get involved with trying to separate a lemon from its rind without the right tool. Rind removal can be an ugly, bitter business, which more often results in removing your skin from your finger. (Ask Kim, The Accident-Prone Bartender.) To garnish with a twist, twist the rind over the drink, releasing the lemon oil into the drink, and then run the yellow side of the twist around the lip of the glass. Finally, toss the twisted twist into the drink. To make an orange slice, cut an orange in half, then cut a slice approximately ½ inch thick. Cut the slice in the middle and rest it over the lip of the glass. Cherries are self-explanatory.

Basic Motor Skills

Tending bar does not require advanced manual manipulation, but some basic coordination is necessary. (Ask Kim, The Accident-Prone Bartender.) Opposing digits are helpful, as is the ability to grasp and release and to bend at the elbow. Being able to pour, stir, shake, and strain are definite musts. Advanced skills such as mashing, muddling, or flaming are not recommended for beginners.

A Chauffeur, Cab Fare, or a Designated Driver

Sophisticated saturnalians do not drive drunk. That is why chauffeurs were invented. If you cannot afford to keep one on the payroll, by all means have on hand a ready supply of sober volunteers.

Straight Shooters

The shot is a potent combination of alcohol and mixers expertly blended to produce an ounce and a half of liquid dynamite. To do a shot is not only to drink it, but to join in a ritual of release, the primary goal of which is to get as drunk as possible, as quickly as possible, without getting tossed out of the bar. We've collected the recipes for thirty-eight all-time classics, so now you can manufacture these explosive cocktails at home, or scarier still, actually know what you are drinking when you order a shot at a bar. Warning: This knowledge may prove hazardous to your health, so proceed at your own risk.

Sex on the Beach

1½ OUNCES VODKA

1½ OUNCES PEACH SCHNAPPS

½ OUNCE ORANGE JUICE

½ OUNCE CRANBERRY JUICE

Fill a cocktail shaker ¾ full of ice. Pour ingredients over ice, cover with top or an upside-down glass, and shake vigorously for five seconds. Strain into shot glasses or four-ounce rocks glasses.

Makes two to four servings.

LEGEND AND LORE

A thorough analysis of tavern epos reveals that this shot was first introduced by a an outcast disciple of Zimmerman, named Ralph, who journeyed to Cancun on a

Cheesy Bartender Banter

Work is the curse of the drinking classes. (OSCAR WILDE)

Better empty pockets than empty glasses. (RICH, THE BOWLING ALLEY BARTENDER)

weekend package getaway in search of his mythical blond bijou. Unfortunately, all he scored was the recipe for this shot, which has turned out to be a keystone in the mating rituals of future generations of Zimmermanians, who have used "Hey Baby, how about some sex on the beach?" as an effective pickup line when attempting to make time with their own mythical babes.

SAFETY TIP
Watch out for the undertow.

SOME LESSER-KNOWN SEXY SPINOFFS
Sex on the Median Strip

Sex on AstroTurf

Sex on the E Train

Sex on a Shoestring

Sex on a Godda Da Vida, Baby!

Pithy Classical Allusion

MACDUFF: What three things does drink especially provoke?

PORTER: Marry, sir, nose-painting, sleep, and urine. Lechery, sir, it provokes, and unprovokes; it provokes the desire, but it takes away the performance. . . .
(WILLY SHAKESPEARE)

Slippery Nipple

1½ OUNCES BAILEYS IRISH CREAM

1½ OUNCES SAMBUCA

Fill a cocktail shaker ¾ full of ice. Pour ingredients over ice and cover with top or an upside-down glass. Shake vigorously for five seconds and strain into shot glasses.

Makes two servings.

LEGEND AND LORE

This shot dates back to the fields of ancient Eire. The Celts used this creamy, sweet concoction as a ceremonial libation in their fertility rites. It didn't do much to increase the harvest of Kennebec Reds, but who needs boiled potatoes when you're swimming in eighty-proof mother's milk? Serve this the next time you experience a potato famine and see if anybody complains. If they do, toss them a bag of chips and appoint them your designated driver for the evening.

SAFETY TIP

The ancient Celts never used "How about a slippery nipple" as a pickup line to make time with their bonnie babes, and you shouldn't, either, unless you're packing an enormous shillelagh.

Mal Mots from Bad Girls

I don't feel quite like a woman until I've got my eyes drawn on. I've got a technique that doesn't take any time, and you can do it when you're drunk. (CHRISSIE HYNDE, THE PRETENDERS, 1980)

Historical Fun Fact: The Origin of the Shot

There are many legends associated with the development of the first shot. One popular hypothesis holds that the ancient Egyptians introduced shots to the Western world during the time of the little-known fourth plague, which set upon the land a legion of gourd beetles (also known as mug scarabs), which decimated the entire supply of Egyptian glassware. The resourceful pharaoh, who would not let the people go, mandated that the shells of the dead scarabs be used as drinking receptacles. When you can only drink an ounce and a half of something at a time, it better pack a sphinx-size wallop! So it shall be written, so it shall be done.

Blow Job

2 OUNCES FRANGELICO

2 OUNCES BAILEYS IRISH CREAM

2 OUNCES KAHLUA

WHIPPED CREAM FOR TOPPING

Fill a cocktail shaker ¾ full of ice. Pour Frangelico, Baileys, and Kahlua over ice, shake, and strain into four small-mouth shot glasses (you know, the kind you find at flea markets and garage sales or behind your dad's bar gathering dust, usually emblazoned with the name of some state, national monument, or obscure athletic team). Top with enough whipped cream so that it slops over the sides a bit. Makes four servings.

LEGEND AND LORE

This is a favorite among orally fixated men who have a latent desire to teach their grandmothers how to suck eggs. This little-known pathology associated with a latent Oedipal conflict stems from a deep-seated fear of being absorbed by a devouring mother—and yes, some girls like it too—but that's a couch of a different color.

ETHNOLOGICAL OBSERVATIONS

There are very specific rules about how to do a blow job. You clasp your hands behind your back, bend at the waist at a forty-five-degree angle, and grasp the mouth of the glass with your lips. Next, you tilt your head back and let the creamy liquid flow down your throat. Needless to say, because of the whipped cream floating on the top of this drink, once the glass is released, a certain effect is achieved. If you are wondering just what this effect is, you are either, A) Not old enough to be requesting blow jobs, B) hanging out in the wrong bars, or C) your name is Ralph.

SAFETY TIP
Swallowing is mandatory.

Tootsie Roll

1   OUNCE CRÈME DE CACAO (DARK)
1½ OUNCES VODKA
1½ OUNCES ORANGE JUICE

Fill a cocktail shaker ¼ full of ice. Pour ingredients over ice and cover with top or an upside-down glass. Shake vigorously for five seconds and strain into shot glasses or four-ounce rocks glasses.

Makes two to four servings.

LEGEND AND LORE
This shot tastes just like a Tootsie Roll but won't stick to your dental work!

Naked Aviator

1 ½ OUNCES VODKA

1 ½ OUNCES MIDORI MELON LIQUEUR

1 ½ OUNCES MALIBU RUM

1 ½ OUNCES PINEAPPLE JUICE

Fill a cocktail shaker ¾ full of ice. Pour ingredients over ice and cover with top or an upside-down glass. Shake vigorously for five seconds and strain into shot glasses.

Makes four servings.

LEGEND AND LORE

This shot has been known to inspire even the most chastely earthbound chawbacon to hijack the nearest Piper Cub bound for the wild blue yonder.

SAFETY TIPS

Don't forget your Dramamine.

Historical Fun Fact:
Another Origin of the Shot

Some mixological historians claim that shots are an ancient Chinese secret invented to get back at Westerners for Kung Fu Fighting.

Foreplay

1   OUNCE VODKA
1   OUNCE PEACH SCHNAPPS
1½ OUNCES CRANBERRY JUICE
 ½ OUNCE BLUE CURAÇAO

Fill a cocktail shaker ¾ full of ice. Pour ingredients over ice and cover with top or an upside-down glass. Shake vigorously for five seconds and strain into shot glasses or four-ounce rocks glasses.

Makes two servings.

LEGEND AND LORE

Some experts claim that if Ralph's legendary package getaway had unearthed this shot, he might have come home with more on his arm than a sunburn.

SAFETY TIPS

It is a good idea to have this before ordering Sex on the Beach.

Pithy
Classical Allusion

Lord, make me chaste—but not yet. (ST. AUGUSTINE)

Mind Eraser

1½ OUNCES KAHLUA
1½ OUNCES VODKA
CLUB SODA TO FILL

Fill a ten-ounce glass with ice, pour Kahlua, and layer vodka on top of the Kahlua. Fill the remainder of the glass with club soda and do the shot through a straw in one slurp. The Kahlua on the bottom of the glass helps the medicine go down.

Makes one serving.

LEGEND AND LORE

There's a reason why they call this shot a mind eraser, only we can't remember what it is.

SAFETY TIPS

It is not advisable to take any standard equivalency tests, operate oil tankers, or hold public office while under the influence of this shot.

Facts are stupid things. (RONALD REAGAN)

The Brain Hemorrhage

1   OUNCE STRAWBERRY SCHNAPPS (PEACH IS ALSO QUITE TASTY)

½   OUNCE BAILEYS IRISH CREAM

    DASH OF GRENADINE

Chill schnapps over ice and pour into a shot glass. Using the back of a spoon, pour the Baileys against the spoon so it dribbles into the schnapps. Finish with a few drops of grenadine dribbled freehand in the center.

Makes one serving.

LEGEND AND LORE

This drink is a multimedia event. Not only is it a drink but a piece of performance art. When you add the Baileys to the schnapps, the Baileys coagulates into a cool looking brainy thing. Some of the grenadine falls to the bottom, sometimes taking part of the brain with it. Totally gross! Mapplethorpe's got nothin' on this piece of work!

SAFETY TIP

It's probably not a good idea to look to the NEA to fund any creative projects in this medium.

Cement Mixer

1 OUNCE BAILEYS IRISH CREAM

½ OUNCE ROSE'S LIME JUICE

Put two shot glasses on the bar. Put Baileys in one glass and the Rose's Lime Juice in the other. (See the ethnological observations below for complete directions on what to do—or not do if you're smart—next.)

Makes one serving.

LEGEND AND LORE

This is the official drink of the Brotherhood of Teamsters, who we think are a great group of guys—really. We just adore them—even if a few of them (who shall remain nameless) pantsed the shot girl at the Blue Ball Bar and Grill last Tuesday night because she blew her whistle right in the middle of the second chorus of "Free Bird." It has been suggested that Jimmy Hoffa may have been drinking this shot on the night he disappeared, so either he was feeling his oats and talked some unsuspecting big rig brother into doing this shot, or he made an unsavory crack about Lynyrd Skynyrd. Either way, if we were him, we'd still keep a low profile.

> A man must swallow a toad every morning if he wishes to be sure of finding nothing still more disgusting before the day is over. (CHAMFORT)

Convince an unsuspecting Teamster to put the Baileys in his mouth without swallowing and then add the Rose's. Tell him to swish the mixture around for ten seconds before swallowing. The look on his face is worth a thousand labor concessions as the mixture solidifies in his mouth.

SAFETY TIPS

Savor the moment. It may be your last.

Historical Fun Fact: And Still Another Origin of the Shot

One friend of ours claims that the first shot was actually a government conspiracy designed to force mug manufacturing unions to make unfair concessions in their new labor contract, but this guy is a paranoid schizophrenic and we don't hang around him much anymore. Did you hear that Irwin? The girls that live on East Thirteenth and Avenue A are not your friends.

Dirty Girl Scout Cookie

1 OUNCE KAHLUA
1 OUNCE CREME DE MENTHE (GREEN)
½ OUNCE VODKA
½ OUNCE MILK

Fill a cocktail shaker ¾ full of ice. Pour ingredients over ice and cover with top or an upside-down glass. Shake vigorously for five seconds and strain into shot glasses.

Makes two servings.

LEGEND AND LORE

This shot tastes just like a thin mint Girl Scout cookie, only it packs a wallop, won't give you cavities, and you don't have to buy it from some cloying miniature Avon lady with a merit badge in Annoying.

SAFETY TIPS

Just like the cookies, no one can have just one.

Stupid Stuff to Say While Pounding the Shot

On my honor, I will try, to do my duty, to God and my country. To help other people at all times, to obey the Girl Scout laws. (THE GIRL SCOUT PLEDGE)

Flaming Dr Pepper

1 OUNCE AMARETTO

¼ OUNCE BACARDI 151 RUM

APPROXIMATELY 4 OUNCES BEER

In a twelve-ounce beer glass, pour approximately four ounces of beer, which should fill the glass a little below the halfway point. Set a shot glass next to the beer. Fill the shot glass 3/4 full with Amaretto. Top with Bacardi 151 rum. Do not fill the shot glass all the way to the rim! Light the Bacardi 151 rum on fire and drop it into the beer glass. Drink back in one gulp.

Makes one serving.

LEGEND AND LORE

I'm a pepper, she's a pepper, he's a pepper, you're a pepper, wouldn't you like to be a pepper, too?

SAFETY TIPS

Caving in to peer pressure has resulted in many an unfortunate household accident. In order to avoid setting yourself, your friends, your chia pet, or your cat on fire, do not fill your shot glass full to the rim, and do not drop the shot glass into the beer from a great height, no matter what the other peppers say.

Pithy Classical Allusion

Remember, only you can prevent forest fires.

(SMOKEY THE BEAR)

Dentyne

1 OUNCE RUMPLEMINTZ

1 OUNCE CINNAMON SCHNAPPS

Fill a cocktail shaker ¼ full of ice. Pour ingredients over ice and cover with top or an upside-down glass. Shake vigorously for five seconds and strain into a shot glass.

Makes one serving.

LEGEND AND LORE

This shot tastes just like a stick of Dentyne gum.

SAFETY TIPS

This shot is not recommended for use during office hours as a breath freshener. For this we recommend the Mentos Popper. (See page 44.)

Desert Storm

¾ **OUNCE BAILEYS IRISH CREAM**
¾ **OUNCE KAHLUA**
  APPROXIMATELY 4 OUNCES CLUB SODA
  DASH GRENADINE

Combine Baileys and Kahlua in a shot glass. Pour chilled club soda into a ten-ounce glass to the halfway point or below. Drop the shot glass of Kahlua and Baileys into the club soda. Dribble grenadine into the glass and drink in one gulp.

Makes one serving.

LEGEND AND LORE

This drink got its name because of the effect that is achieved when you drop the shot glass into the club soda. It looks just like a sandstorm or an artillery barrage in the Sahara.

SAFETY TIPS

Drink before the sand settles. War is not pretty.

Stupid Things to Say While Pounding the Shot

"Ready, aim, fire!" or "Lock and load!"

Mud Slide

½ **OUNCE VODKA**

½ **OUNCE KAHLUA**

½ **OUNCE BAILEYS IRISH CREAM**

There are two ways to create this shot. For the anal retentive among us, we can cleanly layer the ingredients to produce a striated effect. Start with Kahlua, then, using the back of a spoon, pour the Baileys against the spoon so that it rests cleanly atop the Kahlua (which is called floating). Next, float the vodka on top of the Baileys. The second and less labor-intensive method is to throw it all into a shaker with ice, toss it around a little, and strain it into a shot glass. I mean, it all ends up in the same place anyway.

Makes one serving.

LEGEND AND LORE

The origins of this shot are about as clear as mud, but Joey the Ice Pick insists that when these liquors are poured one at a time over rocks, it looks just like mud sliding down an icy mountain. We didn't want to break it to Joey (we don't break much to Joey, you should see what this guy can do with an ice pick), but most of us could care less about the landscape. This is why we've completely dispensed with the ice portion of this concoction. It only presents another obstacle on the way to your bloodstream.

SAFETY TIP

Wear your crampons. You can never be sure when the ground under your feet may give way.

Gay and
Amusing Party Games:
One Fat Hen

Here's a drinking game guaranteed
to amuse. Go around a circle and
have each of your friends repeat the
following phrases, adding a new
phrase each time until they are
repeating the entire paragraph.
Anyone who messes up must chug
their whole drink.

1) One fat hen. 2) Coupl'a ducks.
3) Three brown bears. 4) Four
running sheep. 5) Five fat females.
6) Six simple simons sipping
Seagrams by the seashore. 7) Seven
Sicilian sailors sailing the seven seas.
8) Eight cocky sock cutters cockily
cutting socks. 9) Nor am I a fig
plucker nor a fig plucker's son.
10) But I'll keep on plucking figs till
the fig plucker comes.

It is not advisable to play this game
when there are any cocky sock
cutters or fig pluckers in attendance.
You could wind up getting more than
your tongue twisted!

Prairie Fire

1 ½ OUNCES TEQUILA

DASH TABASCO

If you need mixing instructions for this drink, you've been spending too much time on the open prairie. Deal with it, Toto, you're not in Kansas anymore.

Makes one serving.

LEGEND AND LORE

This drink got its name because after you drink it, your breath could start a serious brush fire in any arid ecosystem.

SAFETY TIP

Those who play with fire usually get burned. If after several of these shots, the sot in the spurs next to you offers to carry you back to the lone prairie, it might be a good idea to make sure Joey has his ice pick handy.

Learning to drink is a lot like learning to toss a baton. It's best not to practice around anything breakable. (DANNY, THE BATON-TWIRLING BARTENDER)

Words to live by, Danny

Snake Bite

1 ½ OUNCES YUKON JACK

1 ½ OUNCES ROSE'S LIME JUICE

Fill a cocktail shaker ½ full of ice. Pour ingredients over ice and cover with top or an upside-down glass. Shake vigorously for five seconds and strain into shot glasses.

Makes two servings.

LEGEND AND LORE

If the serpent in the garden had packed a wallop like this, Adam and Eve might not have been as interested in eating that apple and who knows . . . we might all still be swingin' in the paradise.

SAFETY TIPS

Never, but never, eat of the tree of knowledge of good and evil unless you are prepared to face the fact that you are buck naked in the middle of a garden.

Pithy Anonymous Allusion

How do you like them apples? (ANONYMOUS)

Depth Charge

½ **MUG OF BEER**

1 **OUNCE JACK DANIEL'S**

Pour beer into a mug to the halfway point or lower. Then, fill a shot glass with Jack Daniel's. Drop the shot glass into the beer, and it's bombs away.

Makes one serving.

LEGEND AND LORE

The name of this shot does not mean to imply depth in any spiritual or intellectual sense of the word; rather, it refers to the depths to which one must descend in order to even contemplate creating or ordering such a thing.

ETHNOLOGICAL OBSERVATIONS

This is for the stout of heart who are able and willing to drink this in one pull. He who hesitates gets nauseous. Remember, it's hard to hit a target with a smart bomb from thirty-five thousand feet with your head in the airsick bag.

SAFETY TIP

Look out below!

Dive! Dive! Dive! Dive!

(RON, THE PEARL-DIVING BARTENDER)

B-52

½ **OUNCE KAHLUA**

½ **OUNCE BAILEYS IRISH CREAM**

½ **OUNCE GRAND MARNIER**

This is a layered shot. Pour Kahlua into a shot glass, then, using the back of a spoon, float the Baileys and the Grand Marnier on top in that order.

Makes one serving.

LEGEND AND LORE

This tasty and sweet potation is said to have been created by honorary Private First Class Wing Nut, head bartender at the officers' club in Okinawa. Private Nut is said to have developed a strange and somewhat unsettling attachment to a grounded B-52 bomber parked just outside his barroom window. Rumor has it that he named it Bubba and could often be found tippling this frivolous concoction in the cockpit while simultaneously stroking Bubba's joystick.

SAFETY TIP

There is no such thing as safe sex with a B-52 bomber named Bubba.

> Hibby hibby Ford,
> Hibby Ford
> Hibby, hibby, hibby
> Shake!
> (THE B-52'S, "ROCK LOBSTER")

Woo-Woo

1½ OUNCES VODKA

1 OUNCE PEACH SCHNAPPS

1 OUNCE CRANBERRY JUICE

Fill a cocktail shaker ¾ full of ice. Pour ingredients over ice and cover with top or an upside-down glass. Shake vigorously for five seconds and strain into shot glasses.

Makes two servings.

LEGEND AND LORE

Tavern lore contends that this shot got its name when it was served to Bruce Springsteen at the Stone Pony. After sating his proletarian parch with this refreshing blend, he is said to have exclaimed, "Woo-woo!" Okay, so Bruce isn't the most articulate guy in the world, but hey, who's gonna argue . . . he's The Boss.

SAFETY TIP

Know your limits. Sometimes we all have to retreat and surrender.

Bizarre Bartender Wisdom

My number-one rule is, always keep your eye on the baton, otherwise, you wind up with bruised elbows. (DANNY, THE BATON-TWIRLING BARTENDER)

You go, girl!

Liquid Heroin

1   OUNCE JAGERMEISTER
1   OUNCE RUMPLEMINTZ
1   OUNCE BACARDI 151 RUM

Fill a cocktail shaker ¾ full of ice. Pour ingredients over ice and cover with top or an upside-down glass, shake vigorously for five seconds and strain into shot glasses.

Makes two servings.

LEGEND AND LORE

This shot got its name because when properly mixed, it resembles a substance that has been cooked in a spoon over a tentative flame in some dingy squat in New York's East Village prior to the gentrification of Tompkins Square.

SAFETY TIPS

Hey kids, just say no!

Pertinent Vocabulary Word

SQUAT\'skwät\vb: 1. Sit on one's haunches or heels. 2. To crouch down and cower, as an animal. 3. To settle on land esp., public or new land, without title, right, or payment of rent.

Kamikaze

2   OUNCES VODKA

½   OUNCE ROSE'S LIME JUICE

½   OUNCE TRIPLE SEC

Fill a cocktail shaker ¾ full of ice. Pour ingredients over ice and cover with top or an upside-down glass. Shake vigorously for five seconds and strain into shot glasses.

Makes two servings.

LEGEND AND LORE
Tora, tora, tora!

SAFETY TIP
If you're pledging a fraternity and this shot is served to you in the big gulp size, we recommend you consider rooming at the dorms where you don't have to pay your rent with brain cells.

Lame Fraternity Song to Sing While Pounding the Shot

Oh it's beer, beer, beer, that makes you want to cheer
In the halls, In the halls, In the halls, In the halls.
Oh it's beer, beer, beer, that makes you want to cheer, in
the halls of S.A. Halls of S.A.E. (AN S.A.E. PLEDGE SONG OF
UNKNOWN AND OBVIOUSLY IGNOMINIOUS ORIGIN)

Can you say "Summa cum laude"?—
We didn't think so.

Watermelon Shot

1½ OUNCES VODKA

1 OUNCE MIDORI MELON LIQUEUR

1½ OUNCES CRANBERRY JUICE

Fill a cocktail shaker ¾ full of ice. Pour ingredients over ice and cover with top or an upside-down glass and shake vigorously for five seconds and strain into shot glasses.

Makes two servings.

LEGEND AND LORE

This shot tastes just like a watermelon only without the seeds, and has become America's favorite Fourth of July shot. Normally, a whole batch of watermelon shots are mixed ahead of time and served in a hollowed-out watermelon. That's our kind of Yankee doodle dandy!

SAFETY TIP

Do not operate near an open flame.

Alabama Slammer

1   OUNCE SOUTHERN COMFORT

1   OUNCE SLOE GIN

1   OUNCE ORANGE JUICE

Fill a cocktail shaker ¾ full of ice. Pour ingredients over ice and cover with top or an upside-down glass. Shake vigorously for five seconds and strain into shot glasses.

Makes two servings.

LEGEND AND LORE

Now you know why sweet home Alabama is so sweet. They're all tanked on this toxic punch.

SAFETY TIP

This could have been one of the things that drove old Dixie down.

Other Great Things to Come out of Alabama

- *Deliverance*
- *The Dukes of Hazard*
- Alabama (the band)
- Assorted reptiles
- Fatback
- Collard greens
- Lynyrd Skynyrd
- That frequent flier angel from Montgomery
- Really, really big (and we mean YUUUGE) mosquitoes
- The Crimson Tide.

Red Death

2 OUNCES VODKA

1 OUNCE SOUTHERN COMFORT

1 OUNCE SLOE GIN

½ OUNCE ROSE'S LIME JUICE

½ OUNCE TRIPLE SEC

1 OUNCE ORANGE JUICE

Fill a cocktail shaker ¾ full of ice. Pour ingredients over ice and cover with top or an upside-down glass. Shake vigorously for five seconds and strain into shot glasses or four-ounce rocks glasses.

Makes two to four servings.

LEGEND AND LORE

This is a combination of a Kamikaze and an Alabama Slammer developed by Dave the bartender at the now extinct New York City bar, Name This Joint, which never did find a name or a stable customer base, maybe because the people who were drinking these house specialties couldn't remember *their own* names the next morning let alone the name of this bar, which never had a name in the first place. Duh!!!

SAFETY TIP

The frightening thing is, even though the bar is gone, Dave is still out there somewhere.

Orgasm

- 1 OUNCE BAILEYS IRISH CREAM
- 1 OUNCE GRAND MARNIER
- 1 OUNCE FRANGELICO

Fill a cocktail shaker ¾ full of ice. Pour ingredients over ice and cover with top or an upside-down glass. Shake vigorously for five seconds and strain into shot glasses.

Makes two servings.

LEGEND AND LORE
This shot is best experienced simultaneously.

SAFETY TIP
Multiple orgasms are not a myth.

Tasteless Bartender Humor

Mi idea de una diosa diez puntos es una mujer que tiene un metro altura, sin dientes, con una cabeza plana donde se puede meter su cerveza fria.

Translation: My idea of a perfect ten is a three-foot-tall woman with no teeth and a flat head so you can put your beer down. (RICARDO PANADERO, THE BILINGUAL BARTENDER)

Mango

1½ OUNCES VODKA
1 OUNCE MIDORI MELON LIQUEUR
½ OUNCE ORANGE JUICE
½ OUNCE CRANBERRY JUICE
½ OUNCE PINEAPPLE JUICE

Fill a cocktail shaker ¾ full of ice. Pour ingredients over ice and cover with top or an upside-down glass. Shake vigorously for five seconds and strain into shot glasses or four-ounce rocks glasses.

Makes two to four servings.

LEGEND AND LORE

This was created by Steven Eads of Lucy's Surfeteria in New York City. Steven was a renowned sidekick of Bruce Willis (by the way, Bruce was known to stop by in the wee hours for a taste of the tropics). Steven went on to such heights of fame as training Tom Cruise for his role in *Cocktail* and last we heard, was still at Bruce's heel, only, ever since *Die Hard*, they don't have to look for their dose of the tropics in a shot glass.

SAFETY TIP

Remember, there's only three little letters separating mango from mangled.

Bon Mots from the Swingin' Set

The whole world is three drinks behind. (HUMPHREY BOGART)

Melon Ball

2 OUNCES VODKA
1 OUNCE MIDORI MELON LIQUEUR
1 OUNCE ORANGE JUICE

Fill a cocktail shaker ¾ full of ice. Pour ingredients over ice and cover with top or an upside-down glass. Shake vigorously for five seconds and strain into shot glasses.
Makes two servings.

LEGEND AND LORE
Melons are not just for breakfast anymore.

SAFETY TIP
This breakfast of champions is not recommended for Olympic athletes in training or anyone else who requires basic motor coordination in their day-to-day life.

It's all in the wrist. (DANNY, THE BATON-TWIRLING BARTENDER)

Do it, Danny, blow my mind out.

Russian Quaalude

1 OUNCE RUSSIAN VODKA

1 OUNCE FRANGELICO

1 OUNCE BAILEYS IRISH CREAM

Fill a cocktail shaker ¾ full of ice. Pour ingredients over ice and cover with top or an upside-down glass. Shake vigorously for five seconds and strain into shot glasses.

Makes two servings.

LEGEND AND LORE

The Russian Quaalude may have been instrumental in bringing about the end of the Cold War. It is a little-known fact that in Moscow *Glasnost* is an idiomatic expression that roughly translates as "Gimme another one of those Quaaludes with a beer back." Who could consider pushing the button after a few of these? Who could even see the button? Okay, it's red, but so are a lot of things, like maraschino cherries, grenadine, the bartender's nose . . . You getting my drift comrade? Strike a blow for world peace. Do a Quaalude.

SAFETY TIP

Don't ever drink these while Der Kommissar's in town.

Tequila Popper

1½ OUNCES TEQUILA

1   OUNCE 7UP (OR GINGER ALE)

Pour tequila and 7UP in a four-ounce rocks glass. Place two bar napkins over the mouth of the glass. Put your hand over the napkin and grasp the mouth of the glass tightly so that you make a seal. Raise and slam the glass on the bar. The drink should fizz up like Alka-Seltzer, and while it's fizzing, you down it in one pull.

Makes one serving.

LEGEND AND LORE

This shot was originally developed by the ancient Aztecs as a primitive biological weapon designed to stave off the invasion of the conquistadors. The Aztecs hoped that after three or four of these, the Spaniards would be too polluted to climb the steps and sack the temple.

ETHNOLOGICAL OBSERVATIONS

Montezuma's Revenge, a remote tequila joint located somewhere in the rain forests of the Yucatan, still performs the ancient ritual associated with this shot. Chairs are piled one on top of the other until a tower is created tall enough for the fearless tequila popper drinker to climb to the top and add his or her name to the list of conquered conquistadors on the ceiling. It is curious to note that in this particular bar, a tequila popper is called a tequila slammer, not because of the noise the glass makes on the bar but because of the noise the drinkers' heads make on the floor when they fall off the chairs.

SAFETY TIP

You better think twice next time you contemplate invading a "primitive society" with a cultural sophistication that far exceeds your own linear, Western conceptions of the world. But if you must, at least remember to bring your crampons. Despite its rich cultural heritage, the Yucatan is not known for the stability of its government or its bar furniture.

Stupid Stuff to Say
While Pounding the Shot

One tequila
Two tequila
Three tequila
Floor!

Pineapple Bomber

2 OUNCES VODKA
1 OUNCE PINEAPPLE JUICE

Fill a cocktail shaker ¾ full of ice. Pour ingredients over ice and cover with top or an upside-down glass. Shake vigorously for five seconds and strain into shot glasses.

Makes two servings.

LEGEND AND LORE

While the above recipe is an instant gratification version, Max the Moroccan tells us that at his New York City club, Max NYC, he adds his own personal touch to this shot by steeping the vodka in a large glass bell jar with fresh pineapple slices. The result is not only intoxicating but delicious, and that's not just because Max is the guy behind the bell jar.

SAFETY TIP

Although the vodka resulting from this steeping method is smooth and has lost much of its kick, the pineapples are murder!

Other Stuff You Can Soak in Alcohol

- Cherries in vodka
- Oranges in tequila
- Peaches in white wine
- Cake in rum
- Your potential in just about anything eighty proof or over

Flaming Lemon Drop

1 ½ OUNCES ABSOLUT CITRON

1 LEMON WEDGE

½ TEASPOON SUGAR

DASH BACARDI 151 RUM

Pour vodka into a shaker ¾ full of ice. Swirl shaker for five seconds and strain vodka into a shot glass. Dip lemon wedge in sugar and lay on rim of shot glass. Drizzle rum over the sugared lemon and light. Take lemon in hand, down the shot, and then suck on the lemon.

Makes one serving.

LEGEND AND LORE

It is true that sugar helps the medicine go down.

SAFETY TIP

It is also true that Bacardi 151 rum helps the medicine go down. But for God's sake, don't make the same mistake Ralph did. Wait till the flame goes out before you suck the lemon.

Stupid Bartender Tricks

Hey kid, your head's on fire.

(KIM, THE ACCIDENT-PRONE BARTENDER)

The Spitball

1½ OUNCES VODKA

2 OUNCES ORBITZ

Fill a cocktail shaker ¾ full of ice. Swirl gently for three seconds. Remove ice with a spoon and pour into a four-ounce rocks glass.

Makes one serving.

LEGEND AND LORE

We're not sure if you can get this newest technology from the Clearly Canadian Beverage Company, but they are test marketing the stuff here in New York, and we've had a blast. You should see the look on people's faces when they get a mouthful of those floaties. Orbitz is a lot of really sweet liquid with these hunks of God-knows-what suspended in it. So it's kind of an eating thing and kind of a drinking thing all at the same time, and the floaties can also double as spit balls.

SAFETY TIP

Don't spit floaties at the bartender.

Bar Slop

2 OUNCES BAR SLOP

Dip shot glass into bar slop bucket, close your eyes, and pound.

Makes one serving.

LEGEND AND LORE

For those of you who don't know, bar slop is the left-over drinks that are thrown into a bucket that sits under the bar sink. You know, the one where they pour what's left of everybody's drink all night long, until by the end of the evening, it's become this pinkish brown kind of toxic waste looking stuff with an occasional bar straw or cigarette butt floating at the top.

SAFETY TIP

This is only for the brave of heart and the recently vaccinated.

Gay and Amusing Party Games: Hi, Jerry

Here's yet another gay and amusing drinking game. Watch an episode of Seinfeld. Every time a character says "Jerry," everybody has to take a sip of their drink. Every time a character says "Hi, Jerry," everybody has to guzzle their whole drink, and if Kramer takes a pratfall after he says "Hi, Jerry," everybody has to guzzle two drinks in a row.

Mentos Popper

(a.k.a. The Freshmaker)

**1½ OUNCES CHILLED PEPPERMINT
SCHNAPPS
1 OUNCE CLUB SODA**

Pour schnapps and club soda into a four-ounce rocks glass. Place two bar napkins over the mouth of the glass. Put your hand over the napkin and grasp the mouth of the glass tightly so that you make a seal. Raise and slam the glass on the bar. The drink should fizz up like Alka-Seltzer, and while it's fizzing, you down it in one pull.

Makes one serving.

LEGEND AND LORE

Remember, nothing gets to you: you stay fresh and cool and full of life with Mentos fresh.

SAFETY TIPS

If you're double-parked and two beefy Eurotrash under-fives pick up your Citröen, they will probably be more interested in a towing fee than your breath mint—and they probably don't take American Express, either. It is wise to remember at this moment that hard cash is the universal language.

The Mikey Special

2 OUNCES ABSOLUT CITRON VODKA

½ OUNCE CRANBERRY JUICE

½ OUNCE GINGER ALE

Fill a cocktail shaker ¾ full of ice. Pour vodka and cranberry juice over the ice, cover with top or an upside-down glass, and shake vigorously for five seconds. Strain into shot glasses and top with ginger ale.

Makes two servings.

LEGEND AND LORE

He likes it. . . . Hey Mikey!

SAFETY TIP

This shot does not supply any of the essential nutrients necessary for a well-balanced diet like niacin, thiamine, or riboflavin, but it does do wonders for your attitudinal requirements.

Pertinent Vocabulary Word

RIBOFLAVIN \ ri-bə-'flā -vən\ n: A compound made from Ribose, $C_{17}H_{22}N_4O_6$, a factor of the vitamin B complex essential for growth, found in milk, fresh meat, eggs, leafy vegetables, etc., or made synthetically and used to enrich prepared foods.

The Crest Shot
(Four Out of Five Dentists Approve)

1 OUNCE VODKA
½ OUNCE CRÈME DE MENTHE (GREEN)
½ OUNCE BLUE CURAÇAO
1½ OUNCES MILK

Fill a cocktail shaker ¾ full of ice. Pour ingredients over ice and cover with top or an upside-down glass. Shake vigorously for five seconds and strain into shot glasses.

Makes two servings.

LEGEND AND LORE
Crest has been shown to be an effective decay-preventing dentifrice when used in a conscientiously applied program of oral hygiene and regular professional care.

SAFETY TIPS
Look Ma, no cavities!

Stupid Bartender Tricks

I was in a toothpaste-eating contest once. The gig was whoever threw up harder and longer was the winner. And I won. I'm lucky with those kinds of things. (KIM, THE ACCIDENT-PRONE BARTENDER)

Come in a Hot Tub

1½ OUNCES VODKA
1½ OUNCES TRIPLE SEC
DASH OF MILK

Fill a cocktail shaker ¾ full of ice. Pour vodka and triple sec into shaker over ice. Cover with top or bar glass and shake vigorously for five seconds and strain into shot glasses. Dribble a few drops of milk into each glass.

Makes two servings.

LEGEND AND LORE
Ralph? . . . Is that you?

SAFETY TIP
Didn't we read somewhere something about hot tubs and male virility?

Gay and Amusing Party Games and Holiday High Jinks: The Drinking Grinch

Here's a festive party idea. Watch The Grinch Who Stole Christmas, and every time anybody says "Who," everybody has to down their eggnog. Merry Christmas!

Milk Shake

1   OUNCE VODKA

1   OUNCE KAHLUA

1   OUNCE AMARETTO

1   OUNCE FRANGELICO

2   OUNCES MILK

Fill a cocktail shaker ¾ full of ice. Add ingredients and cover with top or an upside-down glass. Shake vigorously for five seconds and strain into shot glasses or four-ounce rocks glasses.

Makes three to four servings.

LEGEND AND LORE

It's important to nurture our inner children every once in a while.

SAFETY TIP

When you find yourself considering a lifetime membership to the Gymboree, it's time to start nurturing the outer adult.

Cheesy
Bartender Banter

The other day this lady came into the bar, see, and right away I know she's gonna be trouble 'cause she's gotta think about what she wants to drink, and anybody's gotta think about it doesn't belong in my bar in the first place. Then she orders a Brandy Alexander, of course, and I know I got problems right then because anybody mixes a dairy product with their hooch is an amateur. Okay, so I'm mixing her drink and all of a sudden she says, "Hey, Barkeep! That cream is marked April. It is now July." So I say, you know, "So?" And she says, "So, it's past its expiration date." So I say, "Lady, so are you, but you don't hear me complainin'."

—AS TOLD BY JOEY THE ICEPICK,
BARTENDER AT THE
BLUE BALL BAR AND GRILL

Three

Staken Not Shirred— The Neo- Martini

A martini is not just a cocktail, it's an American icon; a symbol of elegance, sophistication, and élan. Sadly, the martini suffered a career setback as a consequence of a very unglamorous but fortunately short-lived national fixation with health, wealth, and happiness. Fortunately, on the cusp of the new millennium, such pedestrian concerns have fallen by the wayside and we are pleased to report that the martini has made a meteoric comeback. Once again the few and the fabulous have developed a taste for this legendary, bittersweet draught of ice cold, expertly agitated juniper juice. Today, in cozy lounges, bereted bon vivants and demimondaines recline, supine, in overstuffed divans, sipping from an endless collection of variations on a main martini theme. So, straight from the bohemian grottos of urban hypnotica . . . meet the neo-martini.

Music to Drink
Martinis to Volume 3
Suave, Sleekly Urbane Mix

As Time Goes By, Harry Nilsson

One Note Samba/Spanish Flea, Sergio Mendes &
Brasil 66

Now's the Hour, Martin Denny

Baia, Esquivel

Nassau (from the motion picture *Thunderball*),
John Barry

So Tinha de Ser Com Voce, Elis Regina

Samba di Aviao, Enoch Light & His Orchestra

Until the Real Thing Comes Along, Dean Martin &
the Nelson Riddle Orchestra

Take 5, Dave Brubeck Quartet

Who's Sorry Now?, Esquivel

The Classic Martini

2⅔ OUNCES GIN

1⅓ OUNCES DRY VERMOUTH

LEMON TWIST

The act of making the perfect martini has been elevated to an act of spiritual significance virtually on a par with transubstantiation. While we are not touched by the divine and have never managed to turn water into wine, we have been known to mix a pretty good martini now and again, and here's how we do it. You begin with a cocktail shaker, preferably made of metal. Fill the shaker three-quarters full of ice. Many insist that spring water ice be used to avoid polluting the virgin confluences with tap water impurities, but this is optional. Next you have to make a decision. If you want a dry martini, you have three options. One, you can pour ½ ounce vermouth over the ice, rinse the ice with the vermouth to scent the cubes, and then pour off the vermouth. For a very dry martini you can either shoot a few drops of vermouth over the shaker or simply pass the bottle over the top of the shaker. For a classic martini, pour 1⅓ ounces vermouth into the shaker and do not pour it off. Next, add 3 ounces of gin (or vodka) to the vermouth or vermouth rinsed, or virgin cubes and cover the shaker. Now you have to make another decision. Do you want your martini stirred, or do you want it shaken? Most martini connoisseurs insist that stirring bruises the gin, and so the generally accepted method of martini preparation involves shaking the shaker langorously rather than vigorously, for eight shakes, until the shaker is so cold that your hand almost sticks to it. Then pour into a martini glass that has been chilling for at least twenty minutes. Finally, you must decide whether you want to garnish in the classic style with a twist, be rebellious and opt for an olive, or make a Gibson, which is merely a martini garnished with a cocktail onion. The key to martinis is expert agitation and arctic chill. Good luck.

STORYTIME FOR SWINGERS

Gather round, swingers, B-girls. Come join the circle and cross your legs Indian-style. It's time for storytime, baby.

*G*wendolyn toyed nervously with the heart-shaped locket resting quietly in the delicate hollow of her throat. The blue damask of her ball gown, so like the one she had worn that fateful day in Paris, whispered as she paced, articulating her agitation in soft, silken syllables. Where could Henri have got to? The rest of their lives depended on this night. She had spent many frantic days preparing, and now everything was ready: the candlelight, the haunting, overwrought string motif, the classic martinis, and two completely credible forged letters of transport. But now Henri was late, and timing was everything. Five minutes longer, and her carefully choreographed conspiracy wouldn't amount to a hill of beans. They would certainly miss the plane to Lisbon. The string motif would crescendo before the denouement, and most unimaginable of all, the martinis would be warm.

MORAL OF THE STORY

In desert climes where time has a tendency to go by, it's best to drink your martinis on the rocks.

Let's get out of these wet things and into a dry martini. (ROBERT BENCHLEY)

The Origin of the Martini

The origin of the martini is a matter of much controversy. Some claim that it was invented by Professor Jerry Thomas, head bartender at New York's Knickerbocker Hotel, who also invented the world-famous Blue Blazer. The story goes that a thirsty gold miner slammed a nugget down on the bar and demanded a drink. Professor Thomas invented a drink in his honor, naming it after the thirsty miner, whose name was Julio. Hey, after a few stiff Professor Thomas specials, what's in a name, anyway? Who can even remember names, theirs or anybody else's?

Cosmopolitan

3 OUNCES ABSOLUT CITRON
¾ OUNCE CRANBERRY JUICE
   DASH FRESH LIME JUICE
   LEMON TWIST

Pour Absolut, cranberry juice, and lime juice into a cocktail shaker over ice, gently agitate, and strain into a four-ounce, chilled martini glass. Garnish with a twist of lemon.

ICONOGRAPHY

This is a favorite martini among urban pseudosophisticates who like their clothes black, their vodka pink, and do things like design web sites for a living.

CULTURAL RESONANCE

Exercise caution when interacting with trendoid gearheads who pepper their patter with terms like *pixel* and *vaporware*. They are a relatively new technology, and the manufacturer hasn't gotten all the bugs out yet.

Bon Mots from the Swingin' Set

I drink too much. Last time I gave a urine sample there was an olive in it. (RODNEY DANGERFIELD)

The James Bond Martini

2½ OUNCES GIN
1   OUNCE VODKA
½ OUNCE BLONDE LILLET
LEMON TWIST

Pour gin, vodka, and Lillet into a cocktail shaker over ice, shake, and strain into a four-ounce, chilled martini glass. Garnish with a twist. **Remember, this drink is shaken, never stirred.**

ICONOGRAPHY

James Bond was the first modern man, able to cross continents, operate sophisticated gadgetry, eat in exotic restaurants without once using the wrong utensil, and consistently demand and get a perfectly executed martini. James Bond, like his drink, is an icon, a modern symbol of power and sophistication. James named his martini the Vesper, after a leggy Latvian spy with whom he would while away many a violet hour sipping his perfectly executed potation and basking, no doubt, in the glow of her mellow thighs tucked seductively beneath some high-concept combination leather/polyurethane number inspired by a twisted Hollywood designer's wildest bondage fantasies. Vesper, unfortunately, did not survive as long as the reputation of the drink that was named for her, and Bond lore has it that when she died, James switched to bourbon, which demonstrates that the first modern man was not only suave, elegant, and culturally flexible, but able to make sacrifices in the service of a relationship.

CULTURAL RESONANCE

The next time you come across a leggy Latvian spy in a combination leather/polyurethane cat suit, it might be wise to check and make sure she's only got two legs under her skirt before naming your favorite drink after her. Modern men, like the times, they are a-changin'.

I never have more than one drink before dinner. But I do like that one to be large and very strong and very cold and very well made. I hate small portions of anything, particularly when they taste bad. This drink's my own invention. I'm going to patent it when I can think of a good name. (JAMES BOND, *CASINO ROYALE*, BY IAN FLEMING)

Sunset Martini

3½ OUNCES STOLICHNAYA OHRANJ
½ OUNCE DRY VERMOUTH
DASH ANGOSTURA BITTERS
ORANGE TWIST

Pour Stolichnaya, vermouth, and bitters into a cocktail shaker with ice, stir, and strain into a four-ounce, chilled martini glass. Garnish with a twist of orange.

STORYTIME FOR SWINGERS

*M*arika gazed pensively across the bay as the Northern sun painted the midnight waters of the Volga a nostalgic umber. She took a tentative sip of her sunset martini and thought of Leonid. How brave he had been, and how handsome in his uniform and high sable hat the day he left her forever. She remembered watching him disappear across the steppes, his shoulders braced, his red cloak whipping in the first breezes of a storm of national unrest that would one day engulf them all. But before, in that brief Prague spring, when the tanks had been garlanded in lilies, the cafés crowded with excited dreamers, and the gin scented with orange and bitters, they had thought they would live forever. Marika raised her glass to the dying light. "To Leonid," she whispered, "and to life everlasting." She drained her cup to the dregs and looked to the grizzled Czarist behind the bar. "Nikolai Alexandropov," she said significantly, "you are old and have seen many things. Surely you can tell me."

"I see a great question in your eyes," said Nikolai, "and I will help you if I can. What is it, Masha? What do you want to know?"

"What I want to know is," said Marika, her eyes growing leaden with the weight of her question, "who do you have to fuck around here to get another sunset martini?"

MORAL OF THE STORY

Only toxic waste and Russian vodka live forever.

Pithy Classical Allusion

Under a bad cloak there is often a good drinker.
(CERVANTES, *DON QUIXOTE*)

The TNT-ini

3   OUNCES GIN
1   OUNCE DRY VERMOUTH
    PICKLED JALAPEÑO

Pour gin and vermouth into a cocktail shaker with ice, stir, and strain into a four-ounce, chilled martini glass. Garnish with a pickled jalapeño.

ICONOGRAPHY

It should be noted that this is not—we repeat, not—a recipe for the creation of an explosive device.

CULTURAL RESONANCE

Just to be on the safe side, don't order this around any disaffected mountain men with advanced degrees in mathematics from Ivy League institutions.

Fibber Magee

2¾ OUNCES GIN
¾ OUNCE SWEET VERMOUTH
½ OUNCE GRAPEFRUIT JUICE
DASH BITTERS

Pour into a cocktail shaker with ice, stir, and strain into a four-ounce, chilled martini glass. Garnish with a twist of lemon.

ICONOGRAPHY

Who was Fibber Magee, anyway? Wasn't he on the radio or something? You know, like in the dark ages when nobody knew where Car 54 was, or the identity of that masked man, except this like totally annoying know-it-all shadow guy who laughed really weird. I mean, this was state-of-the-art entertainment. No wonder this poor jamoke was mixing sweet vermouth and grapefruit juice. He had to do something for kicks.

CULTURAL RESONANCE

If you can't get your MTV, reach for a Fibber Magee.

Another Origin of the Martini

Other historians claim that the famous Martini di Arma di Taggia, an immigrant bartender, invented the martini, which seems to make more sense phonetically than the Julio story.

The Eclipse

3 OUNCES GIN
GRENADINE
OLIVE
ORANGE TWIST

Place an olive in bottom of a four-ounce, chilled martini glass. Pour grenadine to cover. Pour gin into cocktail shaker over ice and shake. Strain slowly into glass to layer on top of grenadine. Garnish with a twist of orange.

ICONOGRAPHY

This drink is a metaphor for the eclipse of the glowing orb of Western world dominance as it is slowly submerged in the cold clear gin of the East. And if you think that's a potent image, wait till you get a load of what a grenadine-covered olive tastes like.

CULTURAL RESONANCE

One bad olive can spoil the whole drink, girl.

The Prairie Martini

3¼ OUNCES TARKHUNA VODKA
¾ OUNCE DRY VERMOUTH
LIME TWIST

Pour into a cocktail shaker with ice, stir, and strain into a four-ounce, chilled martini glass. Garnish with a twist of lime.

STORYTIME FOR SWINGERS

Buck wiped the dust of the Texas panhandle from his brow with a frayed bandanna. He squinted into the relentless prairie sun setting behind the makeshift oil rig that would one day bring in a gusher and transform his meager circumstances. Then he'd show them; he'd show them all, especially Loretta down at the Lubbock Shake 'N Strain, who made the best Prairie Martini this side of the Mason-Dixon line, even if she did have a tendency to drop an eyelash in his glass every now and again. And lately she'd taken to carving the lime twists with her teeth. Still, there was something about the way she shaked and strained that Tarkhuna vodka, with just a splash of dry vermouth, and a soggy lime twist, and some special ingredient that nobody'd been able to identify. Loretta said the man who was able to put his finger on her secret ingredient, well that was the man for her, but so far Buck hadn't managed to find the spot.

Truth told, Loretta and Buck were like oil and water. She'd told him she couldn't have eyes for a lowly son of a panhandler like Buck. She had her long, adhesive-resistant lashes set on Jed, the biggest oil tycoon in the county.

When Jed rolled in for his five o'clock martini, Loretta carved his lime with a pearl-handled twist-maker, and Jed's martini glass was always perfectly chilled. Buck sighed and tipped his hat back on his head, staring down at the ground, as if he could see through its parched surface into the core of the earth, where his fortune lay sleeping beneath layers of bedrock, out of his reach.

Buck heard a rumbling, like the sound his stomach would make after a few too many of Loretta's martinis and a side of chili. Then, up from the ground came a bubblin' crude, oil that is . . . baptizing Buck and his claim in a river of prairie mud mixed with pure black gold. As Buck did a jubilant two-step in the ten-karat rain, tasting the bitter Texas tea in his mouth, he realized that the flavor was awfully familiar. Then he hopped into the pickup and gunned it down Lubbock way to let Loretta know he'd just hit a mother lode of her secret ingredient.

MORAL OF THE STORY

There's no secret that a few martinis and a lot of drilling won't unlock.

The Gamekeeper's Martini

3   OUNCES HONEY-HEATHER VODKA

1   OUNCE SWEET VERMOUTH

DASH BITTERS

Pour into a cocktail shaker with ice, stir, and strain into a four-ounce, chilled martini glass.

STORYTIME FOR SWINGERS

Katrinka cantered through the honey heather in search of Scudder, the enigmatic gamekeeper whom her father had forbidden her to see ever again. But she could not resist his dark, misunderstood eyes or his aquiline face, carved into impossible angles by some unidentified ethnic ancestry, which some in the village claimed had something to do with his father's forays into the fertile deltas of occupied India. Nor could she resist those yummy martinis that he scented with wild heather, sweet vermouth, and the bitters of his broken heart, and served to her in his humble cottage at the outskirts of her father's preserve. She came upon him by a lily lake, poised over a rain barrel, bathing himself intently, still as a woodland creature, the lather clinging to the most improbable swells and hollows of his body.

"Alec," said the woman, dismounting and running to him, breathless with the exertion of the ride, the heat of the day, and all that incredible lather, "I had to see you. I don't care what Daddy says. You can't go; not now. Not, when the lilies are on the lake and the young birds just ready to spring tentatively into life metaphorically foreshadowing my own sensual rebirth. And besides, there's a fresh batch of honey-heather vodka just begging to be shaken and not stirred."

The man draped a towel around his waist, which hugged his virile loins just so, and shrugged his powerful shoulders. "There na I can do, lass. The world's come looking for me an' I've ha' done wi' it. There's na more to say except fare thee well. But I'll miss the sweet swell of y'an, and the young bawds, but there it is. The world's got no place for tenderness nor love, and we'll all be devoured, along with every other gentle living thing, by man's greed and the infernal machine."

"Well, " said Katrinka, eyeing a particularly soapy portion of his leanly muscled leg, "it may be that we are all symbols of a naive utopia marked for destruction in the coming industrial age, but today, while the bubbles still cling to the thigh, what do you say we knock back a few of those 'tini's and do what comes naturally?"

MORAL OF THE STORY
Think globally, drink locally.

Blue Sapphire

3½ OUNCES BOMBAY SAPPHIRE GIN

DASH OF BLUE CURAÇAO

Pour Bombay and a dash of blue curaçao into a cock-tail shaker with ice, stir, and strain into a four-ounce, chilled martini glass.

STORYTIME FOR SWINGERS

Sapphire Jim, a seasoned aristocratic imperialist in the service of Her Majesty the Queen, happened upon an abandoned camp whilst on safari in a remote corner of one of those unpronounceable African countries. There were the usual provisions: a canteen, a muddy rifle, canned meat, a gramophone together with a tasteful selection of fugues, and a case of good gin. Being a seasoned aristocratic im-perialist, Sapphire Jim assumed that whatever he stumbled across whilst on safari belonged to him, and broke immedi-ately into the case of good gin.

As he settled back to enjoy the first of what he promised himself would be several rounds of his plundered spoils, he was struck from behind with the gramophone by a sensitive yet savage hunter with refined sensibilities who found himself at odds with the times in which he lived in general, and gin-swigging British imperialists in particular. The blue blood flowed from Jim's wound, trickling from his head into the martini glass still poised delicately in his hand, pinkie extended, coloring the gin a brilliant, sapphire blue. Dennis, with his novelesque sense of ironic juxtaposi-tion, put a fugue on the turntable, and as the sun set behind the Ngong Hills, he raised a glass to the dying of the light and the birth of the sapphire martini.

MORAL OF THE STORY

If you have a farm in Africa, lock up the gin or keep the gramophone handy.

The Barking Dog

1 ⅓ **OUNCES GIN**

1 ⅓ **OUNCES DRY VERMOUTH**

1 ⅓ **OUNCES SWEET VERMOUTH**

2   **DASHES BITTERS**

LEMON TWIST

Pour gin, dry vermouth, sweet vermouth, and bitters into a cocktail shaker with ice, stir, and strain into a four-ounce, chilled martini glass. Garnish with a twist of lemon.

ICONOGRAPHY

Limit yourself to just a couple of these canine concoctions or you could find yourself lost and dehydrated, woofing pathetically, and ultimately leading your unsuspecting neighbors to the scene of a crime.

CULTURAL RESONANCE

Not now, Kato!

The B.V.D.-tini

1⅓ OUNCES GIN

1⅓ OUNCES RUM

1⅓ OUNCES DRY VERMOUTH

Pour into a cocktail shaker with ice, stir, and strain into a four-ounce, chilled martini glass.

ICONOGRAPHY

For those of you of the Fruit of the Loom/Hanes Her Way generation, a B.V.D. was a popular brand of underwear in the 'forties. Why they chose to name a perfectly palatable martini after a Depression-era undergarment is beyond us. We just don't see the connection. Gin, rum, vermouth . . . Does any of this say bikini brief to you? Us either. So we were thinking, maybe it was a secret code developed during the Second World War to keep the Germans in the neighborhood from figuring out what people were drinking. Or maybe it was like a password among fellow tipplers who had discovered the joys of mixing rum and gin and wanted to be able to identify the other members of their secret and select society. Or maybe the guy who invented it was known for getting smashed and wearing his underwear on his head. Who knows? This is one eternal question that will remain forever obscured by history, but if you're curious, and you happen to see a guy drinking one of these with a pair of Speedos on his head, we suggest you ask him.

CULTURAL RESONANCE

When in NYC, it's best to keep your B.V.D.'s on the Q.T. around the NYPD.

The Bronx Zoo

3 OUNCES GIN

1 OUNCE DRY VERMOUTH

JUICE OF ¼ ORANGE

Pour gin, vermouth, and orange juice into a cocktail shaker with ice, stir, and strain into a four-ounce, chilled martini glass.

ICONOGRAPHY

You don't have to be at the zoo to drink this cocktail, because wherever a group of people are gathered together to drink this martini, there the zoo is also.

CULTURAL RESONANCE

It is useful to bear in mind that zoo animals will do anything for peanuts.

Still Another Origin of the Martini

A group of Anglophile academics claim that the English invented the martini. They believe the name derived from the Martini and Henny Rifle used by the British army between 1871 and 1891, but the British think they invented everything, including civilization as a whole. If you've ever been to a public rest room over there, you'll understand that this is a bit of an overinflated claim, coming from a culture that hasn't even got good plumbing down yet.

The Beanie Martini

3   OUNCES ABSOLUT PEPPAR VODKA

¾   OUNCE DRY VERMOUTH

1   PICKLED STRING BEAN

Pour Absolut and vermouth into a cocktail shaker with ice, stir, and strain into a four-ounce, chilled martini glass. Garnish with a pickled string bean.

STORYTIME FOR SWINGERS

Janet watched with shining eyes as Bennie poured her a martini and placed it carefully on the bar on a scalloped white coaster. How careful he was with each small movement, how deliberate. The perfectly chilled glass placed so precisely in the center of the clean white coaster brought tears to her eyes. For Bennie had not always been a bartender. Once he had been a great pilot, moving fighters across the sky with the same grace and ease that he had waltzed her around the dance floor . . . but that was long ago, before that unfortunate incident with the string beans had changed both of their lives forever.

She knew Bennie blamed himself, but it hadn't been his fault. How could he have known that the munitions supply house he targeted was actually a bean shed? Okay, it had smelled like produce, and had been covered in lima, wax, and string bean vines, but things weren't always what they seemed to be. The enemy was fiendishly clever, and often used string beans in the most insidious ways. He had been acting on a hunch and the hunch went bad, and as a result, the humble villagers had had to live without legumes for the rest of the rainy season. It was this that had caused Bennie to leave the sky forever. Every time he climbed into a cockpit and took hold of the joy stick, he imagined that it was a string bean and developed the shakes so badly that takeoff was impossible. And so he had given up lifting his wings and taken up lifting bottles, serving a pickled string bean in each martini to remind him of his disgrace.

"Bennie," Janet said gently, pulling the string bean out of the bottom of her glass and sucking on it seductively. "You've blamed yourself and hidden from the world long enough. Why don't you take me home now? I'll convince you that your joy stick is not really a string bean, and then maybe we could both take off together."

MORAL OF THE STORY

A bean is a bean is a bean. Sometimes things really are what they seem.

Cajun Martini

3 OUNCES GIN

¾ OUNCE DRY VERMOUTH

DASH TABASCO

SLICED PICKLED RED PEPPER

Pour gin, vermouth, and dash of Tabasco into a cocktail shaker with ice, stir, and strain into a four-ounce, chilled martini glass. Garnish with a sliced pickled red pepper.

STORYTIME FOR SWINGERS

Ten Thumbs Thibedeaux, who most folks in Macon County knew to avoid by a wide margin lest the bad luck that trailed him like shrimp stink would rub off on them, got his first lucky break that Wednesday. The new owner of the Blue Bayou Hash 'N Splash hired Ten Thumbs as the bartender when old Jean Luc Frontisgone finally retired. Practically the whole county banded together to protest the hiring, but the new owner, a bleeding heart Yankee, believed in giving every man his fair shake, even Ten Thumbs, who hadn't shook anything without severing it at the base for the better part of thirty years.

That Friday night, a whole band of folks showed up to see what was going to happen when Ten Thumbs took his place behind the bar in the proximity of several large breakable objects, including an eight-hundred-pound glass chandelier that General Lee had hung from with a lampshade on his head the night before they drove old Dixie down. It was a local treasure, a symbol for the enduring South. The Yankees hadn't been able to put one chip in that chandelier, but folks pretty much figured it wouldn't last five minutes when Ten Thumbs picked up the martini shaker.

The remarkable thing about Ten Thumbs was that he never seemed to notice that disaster followed him like crawfish to a chub net. He thought everybody walked into walls or fell into manholes every now and again. And wasn't glass supposed to be breakable? So while he was secretly a little hurt that folks didn't often ask him over to supper, particularly if the fine china would be in use, he didn't think that his lot was much better or worse than anybody else's in the parish. His self-assurance, which had absolutely no grounding in reality, was almost heroic. And so on that Friday night, when Ten Thumbs picked up the martini shaker for the first time, he did so without giving that great old chandelier above his head a second thought. And he really didn't think twice about things either when the shaker shot out of his hand midshake, which dislodged the liqueur shelf, which dislodged the vat of pickled peppers, which, in its descent, sent the lampshade worn by General Lee himself ricocheting into the suspended glass rack which on its descent snagged one of the hand-carved crystal pendulums at the nadir of the chandelier and brought it down on poor Ten Thumbs's thick head. Ten Thumbs, who, unlike most folks he came into contact with, had a white light around him and never came to any serious harm, picked himself up. He shook the dust from his shoulders and poured the martini, which had somehow managed to remain inside the shaker, only with the addition of one of the pickled peppers that were now garishly festooning the bar. Ten Thumbs tasted his newly invented Cajun Martini and pronounced it delicious. Of course, nobody was sitting on any bar stools for some time to come on account of the glass shards lodged in their rear ends, but by the time Ten Thumbs moved on and began working over at Languedoc's filling station, word had pretty much got around that for once, Ten Thumbs was on to a good thing with those Cajun Martinis. Folks in the parish even said they might pull in every now and again and give Ten Thumbs a shot at gassing up their cars, which was a charitable gesture in the extreme. Of course, that was before the lightning storm that razed the station but left Ten Thumbs able to commute telepathically between this world and the other, which left some folks saying that somebody ought to let paradise know to lock up their breakables.

MORAL OF THE STORY

Accidents don't happen in a perfect world, yet . . .

Gunga Din

3   OUNCES GIN

¾   OUNCE DRY VERMOUTH

¼   OUNCE PINEAPPLE JUICE

     SLICE OF ORANGE

Pour gin, vermouth, and pineapple juice into a cocktail shaker with ice, stir, and strain into a four-ounce, chilled martini glass. Garnish with a slice of orange.

ICONOGRAPHY

Gunga Din was the head bartender at the Bombay Booze 'N Snooze, who invented this martini in order to cope with the great pineapple glut in the year of the big rain. Everyone in the delta agreed that Gunga was really onto something this time. This martini was certainly a lot better than what he invented to cope with the great fruit fly infestation the year before. And pineapples were much easier to skewer on a toothpick.

CULTURAL RESONANCE

In Bombay, catching flies with honey is not necessarily a good thing.

The Knockout

1 OUNCE GIN

1 OUNCE DRY VERMOUTH

1 OUNCE PERNOD

1 TEASPOON WHITE CRÈME DE MENTHE
(OPTIONAL)
MINT LEAVES

Pour into a cocktail shaker with ice, stir, and strain into a four-ounce, chilled martini glass. Garnish with mint leaves.

ICONOGRAPHY

If you're into incoherence or total insensibility, this is the martini for you. More effective than Xanax, Atavan, most livestock tranquilizers, or blows to the head with a blunt object, this drink is guaranteed to put the lights out.

CULTURAL RESONANCE

Close your eyes and see. Just make sure you haven't left any money on the bar.

Bon Mots from the Swingin' Set

I never jog. It's too easy to spill my martini. (GEORGE BURNS)

Negroni

1⅓ OUNCES GIN
1⅓ OUNCES SWEET VERMOUTH
1⅓ OUNCES CAMPARI
LEMON TWIST

Pour gin, vermouth, and Campari into a cocktail shaker with ice, stir, and strain into a four-ounce, chilled martini glass. Garnish with a twist of lemon.

STORYTIME FOR SWINGERS

Isabelle sat languidly at a quiet table in the corner of the hotel's outdoor café. The Negresco, poised gracefully at the nape of the Côte d'Azur, had always been her favorite place to sit, have a Negroni, and page through her dog-eared Proust, remembering her own times past. Invariably, this led to thoughts of Gillaume. How he had loved the old village. Nice had seemed a paradise to him, with its orange roofs and terra-cotta walls, the bright geranium pots, and beveled windows, yellowed with the sea. And the way the water sounded as it ebbed and flowed over the black pebble beach, where sun-kissed bathers reclined in thongs in the remarkable morning light. And the water, how deepest azure, and the bright billowy clouds, the cakey brown patties the dogs left to bake on the bleached boards of the promenade. And the Negresco itself, Nice's crown jewel, sparkling gaily amidst all of this natural splendor.

Yes, Gillaume had seen and loved all of these things, but now he saw nothing, and not only because he had became hopelessly nearsighted as of late, or because of the severed limb, the bouts of amnesia, or the gradually escalating fits of paranoid schizophrenia. Isabelle knew it was more than this, for somehow along the way, Gillaume had lost his zest for living. Isabelle knew also that if anything could reawaken Gillaume's joie de vivre, it would be a Negroni at the Negresco. But it was not to be. The asylum would never let him out again after that unfortunate incident with the condom and the shot glass at the Café Monte Carlo. She sighed and sipped her Negroni when suddenly, a starved, one-armed lunatic began waving his arm so wildly that even the sober French dogs stopped to stare. His face was gaunt, his eyes pleading. In his hand, he held a shot glass.

"Gillaume," cried Isabelle, leaning over the railing, offering him her Negroni. "Drink, *mon cher*, drink." She had forgotten that Gillaume only had one arm, and he wasn't letting go of the shot glass. As she held the glass out to him, he tried to reach out to her, but lost his balance and slipped in a cakey brown patty, which had not yet had the opportunity to bake on the bleached boards of the promenade, and fell into the sea. As he disappeared beneath the azure waves, she considered the exquisite beauty of the scene; the Riviera sun just beginning to set over the Toulousian hills, the cheerful geraniums turning dusky with the onset of evening, Gillaume's one arm thrust out from his watery cradle, the dying light glinting like a beacon from the shot glass as he waved his silent and final farewell.

Isabelle thought, *Isn't that emblematic of the tragedy of life? We are offered a perfectly chilled Negroni, but our pride demands that we hold on to our empty shot glass, and then ultimately, our arrogance amounts to nothing and our fate turns on a misplaced pile of dog doo*. She sat back in her chair, pleased with her Proustian postulates, and ordered another Negroni, paying homage to the poetry of the moment.

MORAL OF THE STORY

When life offers you a Negroni, drink it . . . and when in France, watch where you're stepping!

Kir Martini

3   OUNCES VODKA
¾ OUNCE CRÈME DE CASSIS
LEMON TWIST

Pour vodka into a cocktail shaker with ice, stir, and strain into a four-ounce, chilled martini glass. Pour crème de cassis into glass and garnish with a twist.

ICONOGRAPHY

A kir is traditionally a glass of white wine, or in the case of a kir royale, a glass of champagne with a splash of crème de cassis to give it that rosy, civilized glow. It is an elegant aperitif with a soft finish and is known as a temperate, tasteful concoction, most often ordered by women. The Kir Martini has a similar ladylike feel as a consequence of the dash of crème de cassis in the recipe, but don't let that rosy glow fool you. A Kir Martini will kick your derrière but good, and after a few, your drink won't be the only thing that's flushed.

CULTURAL RESONANCE

Sugar and spice and everything nice are not all that little girls are made of.

Music to Drink Martinis to: Volume 2
Los "Swingers" Mix

As Time Goes By (from the motion picture *Casablanca*), Dooley Thomas

Drinking Again, Aretha Franklin

Triste, Joao Gilberto

Surfboard, Esquivel

Mais Que Nada, Sergie Mendes & Brazil 66

Makin' Whoopee, Bob Thompson, His Choir & Orchestra

Agua De Beber, Antonio Carlos Jobim

What's New, Pussycat? Burt Bacharach

Pearly Shells, Martin Denny

Aguas de Marcos, Elis Regina

Nothin' Can Compare to You (from the motion picture *I'll Take Sweden*), Jimmie Haskell

Florentine Martini

3 OUNCES VODKA

1 OUNCE CAMPARI

LEMON TWIST

Pour vodka and Campari into a cocktail shaker with ice, stir, and strain into a four-ounce, chilled martini glass. Garnish with a twist of lemon.

STORYTIME FOR SWINGERS

I was leaning against the bar in a speakeasy on Fifty-second Street when a girl got up from the table and came over to me. She was small, and blonde, and really knew how to fill out a peplum. "Aren't you Dick?" she asked.

"If you're looking for Dick, you've found your man," I said, transfixed with the way that peplum was showcasing her shapely hips, like whitewalls on a mint-condition Packard. My throat felt dry, and I reached for my glass, but it was empty. That had been happening a lot since I'd arrived in the Big Apple. It had something to do with the grit and the heat and the exorbitant price of bathtub gin on Swing Street. No question about it, a hard-boiled, disillusioned, down-and-out but resonantly poetic Los Angeles dick could get very thirsty in this town. But maybe my luck had just changed. "What are you drinking?"

"Two vodka martinis, please, with a splash of Campari and a twist," she said, turning to the bartender, which gave me a glimpse of the nifty pair of hubcaps she had to go with her whitewalls. "They're called Florentine Martinis," she said, "and actually, that's the reason I'm here. You see, it all began on the Piazza di San Marco, in Italy, when I was just a little girl."

I could see she was warming up for a long, boring story full of shattered dreams, broken promises, and overpriced martinis in some pretentious Mediterranean grotto, but she was buying, so even though I was a gin man, I kept my mouth shut. Us hard-boiled, disillusioned, down-and-out but resonantly poetic Los Angeles dicks know where our bread is buttered. Feigning interest. It's in the job description, right in between fedoras and five o'clock shadows.

"Go on," I said in between sips of frigid pink.

"I'm looking for my father," she said, her eyes clouding with a chance of rain. "I haven't seen him since that last night on the Piazza. He had just ordered his sixth Florentine Martini. I had gone inside to powder my nose, and when I returned, he was nowhere to be found. The only trace of him that remained was his empty glass, and resting in the bottom was a lime squeeze. Do you see?"

"This drink comes with a twist."

"Yes, oh yes," she said, the sun in her eyes coming out from behind the clouds. "I knew you were the right dick for me. "

"Well, misgarnishing is a messy business, and your father was an old man with a bladder full of pink vodka in a town full of canals. There's no telling where he might end up."

"Please," she said, finishing her drink, "you're the only one who can help me. I suggest we start with a reenactment of the evening. It's on me. Bartender, two more Florentine Martinis."

The drinks came, and I took a sip, sighing gratefully. I had to admit, they were beginning to grow on me. "Well," she said, raising her glass and clinking it gently, "will you take my case?"

"Dorothy," I said, downing my second martini and ordering a third, "why not? But first could you point me in the direction of the Little Boys' Canal?"

MORAL OF THE STORY

Thin men should never have more than two martinis.

The Volga Boatman

1⅓ OUNCES RUSSIAN VODKA

1⅓ OUNCES CHERRY BRANDY

1⅓ OUNCES ORANGE JUICE

ORANGE SLICE

Pour vodka, brandy, and orange juice into a cocktail shaker with ice, stir, and strain into a four-ounce, chilled martini glass. Garnish with an orange slice.

Marika walked through the lonely streets in search of the boatman, whom the grizzled Czarist behind the bar had told her would have what she wanted. She spied him poling his boat slowly up the Volga, humming a sad ballad to himself as he made his weary way toward home.

"Comrade," Marika called softly, waving him toward shore. "Nikolai Alexandropov told me that you were the one who has what I am looking for."

"What is it you are looking for, Masha?" asked the boatman, his face hidden in the shadow of his high, sable hat. "Are you, perhaps, searching for me?" The boatman removed his hat, and Marika saw that it was Leonid. He was luminous in the moonlight, beaming at her, looking as handsome and brave as he had that last day on the steppes.

"No," said Marika looking past him toward the silver shaker of martinis resting in the bottom of the boat. "I'm thirsty. Now quit beaming and pour me a drink."

Leonid nodded and helped her aboard, pouring her a hefty Volga Boatman as they sailed into the northern mist and disappeared forever.

MORAL OF THE STORY

Ask not for whom the boat poles, it poles for thee. But hopefully, they'll be serving martinis on board.

Gin stops the bell from tolling. (E. B. WHITE)

The Melontini

3 OUNCES VODKA
1 OUNCE MIDORI MELON LIQUEUR

Pour into a cocktail shaker with ice, stir, and strain into a four-ounce, chilled martini glass.

ICONOGRAPHY
This new miracle martini has been known to stimulate the hormones that induce sleep. It should be mentioned, however, that it does decrease your percentage of deep sleep by 40 percent, which can hasten the aging process; but then again, so does sobriety, so if you ask us, we'll take the aging under the influence option, hands down.

CULTURAL RESONANCE
Sleep my child, and peace attend thee, all through the night.

The Amaratini

3 OUNCES VODKA
1 OUNCE AMARETTO

Pour into a cocktail shaker with ice, stir, and strain into a four-ounce, chilled martini glass.

ICONOGRAPHY
It is said that the addition of Amaretto into a martini adds a little touch love.

CULTURAL RESONANCE

Amaretto is brown, so your drink should be tawny in hue. If there's any white gunky stuff floating around, ask the bartender to go lighter on the amore.

Music to Drink Martinis to:
Volume 3
Ambient, Space-Age Bachelor Pad Mix

Mucha, Mucha-cha, Esquivel

Champagne, My Dear? Jim Backus

Girl From Ipanema, Stan Getz/Joao Gilberto

Jalousie, Esquivel

Look of Love (from the motion picture
Casino Royale), Dusty Springfield, Herb Alpert

Quiet Village, Martin Denny

From Another World, Sid Bass and His Orchestra

Chega de Saudad, Antonio Carlos Jobim

Love Theme (from the motion picture *Carpet Baggers*) Elmer Bernstein

Hotel, (from the motion picture *Hotel*), Carmen McRae, Johnny Keating

Main title (from the motion picture
Ginger and Fred), Nino Rota

Ipcress File, John Barry

Casino Royale, Burt Bacharach

The Chocolate Martini

3 OUNCES VODKA
1 OUNCE WHITE CRÈME DE CACAO
   ORANGE SLICE

Pour vodka and crème de cacao into a cocktail shaker with ice, stir, and strain into a four-ounce, chilled martini glass. Garnish with an orange slice.

ICONOGRAPHY

Ooey, gooey, rich and chewy outside.
Lots of kick your bootie on the inside.

CULTURAL RESONANCE

This kind of chocolate treat can cause more to break out than just blemishes.

Oompah, Loompah. (WILLY WONKA'S TOAST, *CHARLIE AND THE CHOCOLATE FACTORY*, BY ROALD DAHL)

The Drunk Monk

3 OUNCES VODKA

1 OUNCE FRANGELICO

Pour into a cocktail shaker with ice, stir, and strain into a four-ounce, chilled martini glass, and start praying.

ICONOGRAPHY

Celibacy and silence, okay, but nobody said anything about sobriety.

CULTURAL RESONANCE

Sometimes, drinking can be a religious experience. Why, just last night, Ralph swears he saw God. Unfortunately, it turned out to be a traffic cop, and now he's doing major penance. So, just to be on the safe side, the next time you see God on the corner of 42nd Street and 8th Avenue, be sure to hand over your driver's license before kissing the hem of his robe.

Historical Fun Fact

Chartreuse, Benedictine, and Frangelico were all invented by monks . . . It's true!

Th Trini Lopez Memorial Martini

3 OUNCES VODKA

¼ OUNCE MALIBU RUM

SLICE OF PINEAPPLE

Pour vodka and rum into a cocktail shaker with ice, stir, and strain into a four-ounce, chilled martini glass. Garnish with a slice of pineapple.

ICONOGRAPHY

Who is Trini Lopez? We've been on this guy's trail ever since we came upon his memorial martini, and we have yet to have a sighting. First we thought he was a steel conga drum player in some Caribbean band, but that turned out to be Desi Arnaz. Then we thought he was that cute little guy who bites in *Rebel without a Cause*, but that turned out to be Sal Mineo, who wasn't even Latin. Then Rich the bowling alley bar poet told us he thought he was the lithe, sensitive young soldier in *The Dirty Dozen*, and we watched the whole last ten minutes and didn't even see him once. His name did appear in the credits though, so we know he's out there somewhere. So Trini, whoever you are, this one's for you.

CULTURAL RESONANCE

It's comforting to know that you don't have to be a bankable leading man with a high Recognizability Quotient (RQ) to have a drink named after you.

The Au Currant

3 OUNCES ABSOLUT CURRANT

¾ OUNCE CRÈME DE CASSIS

SPLASH OF SODA

Pour vodka into a cocktail shaker with ice, stir, and strain into a four-ounce, chilled martini glass. Add cassis and a splash of soda.

ICONOGRAPHY

This is a martini for state-of-the-art folks who keep up on all the important stuff the rest of us can't quite keep up on. They know that blue nail polish is in, brick brown is out, supermodels are over, male supermodels are not, and that Malibu Barbie is tons cooler than just regular Barbie, because she comes complete with a sense of irony.

CULTURAL RESONANCE

Drink a few of these, and you, too, can turn your mind into a rubbish bin of pop culture detritus. Hey, it beats law or accounting.

The Russian Martini

½   **CUP RUSSIAN VODKA**

     2 SLICES RUSSIAN BLACK BREAD

     4 SLICED DILL PICKLES

ICONOGRAPHY

It is traditional in Russia to pound your vodka warm out of a nondescript cup and then chase the god-awful taste with rich, black bread and dill pickles. They have a no-frills policy over there. It's coarse, but very effective, although the bread has a tendency to stick in your throat like a solid lump of three-day-old borscht.

CULTURAL RESONANCE

To accomplish the Heimlich maneuver, stand behind the choking victim and put your arms around him or her from back to front. Join your hands into a fist at the base of the diaphragm and pump the diaphragm in an upward motion until the black bread is dislodged.

The martini is America's lethal weapon.

(NIKITA KRUSCHEV)

Retro Cocktails— Rococo Recipes from Days of Yore

People have been finding creative ways to get toasted ever since Laird Usquebaugh the merry Celt stumbled headfirst into a cask of overfermented wheat. Of course, fermented wheat may get you twisted in a hurry, but it doesn't taste very good. Neither, for that matter, does bathtub gin, and for these very compelling reasons, people have invented myriad ways to cut the god-awful taste of hooch. The result is a panoply of creative cocktails that reflect both the spirit and the tempo of their times. Here's a few of our favorites.

Scarlett O'Hara

2   OUNCES SOUTHERN COMFORT

1   OUNCE CRANBERRY JUICE

½   OUNCE LIME JUICE

Fill a cocktail shaker ¾ full of ice. Pour ingredients over ice and cover with top or bar glass. Shake with ice for five seconds and strain into a cocktail glass.

HISTORICAL SURVEY

Scarlett O'Hara was not beautiful, but men seldom noticed it when caught by her charms, her independent spirit, and fifty-seven of these shots, which could make even General Grant look fetching in a hoop skirt.

TIME-HONORED TRUTH

Think about it today. Tomorrow you'll have a hangover.

Fiddle dee dee. War, war, war. This talk of war is spoiling the fun at every party this spring. Why, I get so bored of it, I could scream. (SCARLETT O'HARA IN *GONE WITH THE WIND*, BY MARGARET MITCHELL)

Rhett Butler

2 OUNCES SOUTHERN COMFORT
JUICE OF ½ LIME
JUICE OF ½ LEMON
1 TEASPOON CURAÇAO

Fill a cocktail shaker ¾ full of ice. Pour ingredients over ice and cover with top or bar glass. Shake with ice for five seconds and strain into a cocktail glass.

HISTORICAL SURVEY

It is said that this rakish visitor from Charleston was the only buck in the county who could improve on Scarlett's recipe. Unfortunately, Scarlett herself preferred Ashley Wilkes's watery apple cider, which couldn't get a bee buzzing, and eventually, despite the prosperity he and Scarlett enjoyed in a post-Recontructionist South, Rhett didn't give a damn.

TIME-HONORED TRUTH

One should not mix apples and oranges, or anything, when Southern Comfort is involved.

There is a certain swinish comfort in being with a woman who loves you utterly, and respects you for being a fine gentleman—even if she is an illiterate whore. (RHETT BUTLER IN *GONE WITH THE WIND*, BY MARGARET MITCHELL)

Quickie

1½ OUNCES PORT

1½ OUNCES GRAND MARNIER

2   DASHES BITTERS

Fill a cocktail shaker ¾ full of ice. Pour ingredients over ice and cover with top or bar glass. Shake with ice for five seconds and strain into a cocktail glass.

HISTORICAL SURVEY

The appellation of this retro cocktail refers to the relatively short amount of time it takes to mix it, not to any babe action you might be inspired to pursue after drinking two or three. When one considers the provocative blend suggested in this recipe, however, and reflects upon what effect this may or may not have on the central nervous system as well as the lower gastrointestinal tract, it probably would be wise to conclude any romantic encounters in one hell of a hurry, just to be on the safe side.

TIME-HONORED TRUTH

Never tempt fortune, especially when you've been mixing Grand Marnier and port.

When I'm good, I'm very good, but when I'm bad, I'm better. (MAE WEST)

Blue Monday

2 OUNCES VODKA

1 OUNCE BLUE CURAÇAO

Fill a cocktail shaker ¾ full of ice. Pour ingredients over ice and cover with top or bar glass. Shake with ice for five seconds and strain into a cocktail glass.

HISTORICAL SURVEY

Mondays have sucked since forever.

TIME-HONORED TRUTH

Why sing the blues when you can drink them?

On Monday, when the sun is hot
I wonder to myself a lot
Now is it true, or is it not,
That what is which and which is what?
(A. A. MILNE, *WINNIE-THE-POOH*)

The Americano

1 OUNCE CAMPARI

½ OUNCE SWEET VERMOUTH

SODA WATER

ORANGE WHEEL

Fill a cocktail shaker ¾ full of ice. Pour Campari and vermouth over ice and shake vigorously for five seconds. Strain into a cocktail glass and top with soda water. Garnish with an orange wheel.

HISTORICAL SURVEY

This refreshing aperitif, also known as a *neutered negroni,* doesn't pack much of a punch, but for some reason it has been literarily linked to legendary drinkers like Ernest Hemingway and James Bond. The drink was first served in 1861 at Gaspare Campari's bar. Later, the purist Italians, whose national palate was offended by the pollution of Campari with vermouth and soda water, dubbed the drink *The Americano,* at which point it was adopted by the French, who love anything that gives them the opportunity to look down their prodigious Gallic probisci at American tourists.

TIME-HONORED TRUTH

When in doubt, blame it on the French. They probably deserve it.

James Bond had his first drink of the evening at Fouquet's. It was not a solid drink. One cannot drink seriously in French cafés. Out of doors on a pavement in the sun is no place for vodka or whisky or gin . . . No, in cafés you have to drink the least offensive of the musical comedy drinks that go with them, and Bond always had the same thing, an Americano.

—IAN FLEMING, *A VIEW TO A KILL*

The Kangaroo

2 OUNCES VODKA

⅓ OUNCE DRY VERMOUTH

Pour vodka and vermouth into a cocktail shaker with ice, stir, and strain into a four-ounce, chilled martini glass.

ICONOGRAPHY

When down under, fill a bathtub with vodka and float a few olives. . . . it's Australian for martini.

CULTURAL RESONANCE

Take two, they're small.

Absinthe Cocktail

1½ OUNCES ABSINTHE SUBSTITUTE (PERNOD)

1½ OUNCES SIMPLE SYRUP

1 DASH BITTERS

Fill a cocktail shaker ¾ full of ice. Pour ingredients over ice and cover with top or bar glass. Shake with ice for five seconds and strain into a cocktail glass.

HISTORICAL SURVEY

Although absinthe was the reigning feel-good juice of its day, it has since been outlawed, largely because feeling that good can't be legal. Oh, and we also heard something about it growing hair on your brain, but it's like, so? Shouldn't people be allowed to decide for themselves whether or not they want to cultivate a brain coif? It's a free country, right? And if consenting adults want to drink the alcoholic equivalent of neurological Rogaine, then they should be allowed to without moralistic, imperialistic, governmental intervention, right?

Isn't that what democracy is all about?

TIME-HONORED TRUTHS

Remember, the hair of the dog is not always on the other end of your leash.

Absinthe makes the heart grow fonder!

The Bees' Knees

2   **OUNCES GIN**
1   **TEASPOON HONEY**
    JUICE OF ¼ LEMON

Fill a cocktail shaker ¾ full of ice. Pour ingredients over ice and cover with top or bar glass. Shake with ice for five seconds and strain into a cocktail glass.

HISTORICAL SURVEY

Okay, so we can accept that bears shit in the woods and that the pope is probably Catholic, but do bees really have knees? And if a cow laughs, does it shoot milk out of its nose?

TIME-HONORED TRUTH

It's best not to ask questions you don't want to know the answer to.

Between the Sheets

¾   **OUNCE LEMON JUICE**

¾   **OUNCE RUM**

¾   **OUNCE TRIPLE SEC**

¾   **OUNCE BRANDY**

TWIST OF LEMON

Fill a cocktail shaker ¾ full of ice. Pour lemon juice, rum, triple sec, and brandy over ice and cover with top or bar glass. Shake with ice for five seconds and strain into a cocktail glass. Add a twist of lemon.

HISTORICAL SURVEY

This drink got its name because it could be counted on to put people to sleep back in the days before Haldol, Halcyon, Melatonin or Bob Dole provided more effective remedies for insomnia.

TIME-HONORED TRUTH

Campaign speeches and other narcotics should be taken in moderation. They can be addictive and lead to harder drugs.

The Flu

2 OUNCES WHISKEY

1 TEASPOON BRANDY

1 TEASPOON SIMPLE SYRUP

1 TEASPOON LIGHT RUM

JUICE OF ¼ LEMON

SMALL DASH OF GRATED GINGER

Fill a cocktail shaker ¾ full of ice. Pour ingredients over ice and cover with top or bar glass. Shake with ice for five seconds and strain into a cocktail glass.

HISTORICAL SURVEY

This drink got its name because it is a soothing remedy to sip while under the weather. It is rather like the Gilded Age equivalent of NyQuil. It may not cure what ails you, but it'll sure make those sick days in front of the tube with a box of Kleenex and back-to-back *I Love Lucy* reruns a lot more appealing.

An Irish queer: a fellow who prefers women to drink. (SEAN O'FAOLAIN)

TIME-HONORED TRUTH

Be careful when combining syndicated TV and coughing-stuffy-head-fever-so-you-can-rest-medicine. In some cases it can lead to temporary brain death in the intellectually compromised.

The Brainstorm

2 OUNCES WHISKEY

2 DASHES DRY VERMOUTH

2 DASHES BENEDICTINE

TWIST OF ORANGE PEEL

Fill a cocktail shaker ¾ full of ice. Pour whiskey, vermouth, and Benedictine over ice and cover with top or bar glass. Shake with ice for five seconds and strain into a cocktail glass. Garnish with twist of orange.

HISTORICAL SURVEY

Try serving this at your next brainstorming session instead of mineral water and see just how creative your creative department really is!

TIME-HONORED TRUTH

When you walk through a storm, keep your head up off the bar.

Ale man, ale's the stuff to drink
For fellows whom it hurts to think.
(A. E. HOUSMAN)

The Pansy

2   OUNCES ANISETTE

2   DASHES GRENADINE

2   DASHES BITTERS

    LAVENDER PANSY

Fill a cocktail shaker ¾ full of ice. Pour Anisette, grenadine, and bitters over ice and cover with top or bar glass. Shake with ice for five seconds and strain into a cocktail glass. Garnish with a lavender pansy. (Did you ever eat a pansy? Some parts are edible.)

HISTORICAL SURVEY

In the trendy cafés of New York's West Village where this drink originated, it was traditional to whistle a popular show tune of the moment while sipping this color-coordinated concoction.

TIME-HONORED TRUTH

You do know how to whistle, don't you? Put your lips together . . . and blow.

Etymological Fun Fact

The whiskey that evaporates through your pores the next morning is known as osmosis.

Weep No More

1   OUNCE SWEET VERMOUTH

1   OUNCE BRANDY

1   OUNCE LIME JUICE

DASH MARASCHINO

Fill a cocktail shaker ¾ full of ice. Pour ingredients over ice and cover with top or bar glass. Shake with ice for five seconds and strain into a cocktail glass.

HISTORICAL SURVEY

This drink originated during the great Depression as a consolation drink for the bankrupt masses who needed a stiff one before they jumped out the window of the stock exchange. Fortunately, today we don't need liquid comfort in times of economic crisis, because we have had the benefit of Clarence the angel's life-affirming message: "No man is poor who has friends." Yeah, right, Clarence. You're not in Bedford Falls anymore, guy, so what do you say we can the corn and get drunk.

TIME-HONORED TRUTH

Every time a bell rings, Bill Gates makes another billion bucks.

Greta Garbo Cocktail

1½ OUNCES SWEDISH PUNSCH (WE DON'T KNOW WHAT THIS IS, EITHER, BUT IT SOUNDS LIKE IT MIGHT BE BINDING.)

½ OUNCE ORANGE JUICE

½ OUNCE LEMON JUICE

Fill a cocktail shaker ¾ full of ice. Pour ingredients over ice and cover with top or bar glass. Shake with ice for five seconds and strain into a cocktail glass.

HISTORICAL SURVEY

It is said that Greta Garbo was sipping this Scandinavian cocktail when she uttered the immortal line, "I vant to be alone." Given what a couple of these will do on an empty stomach, it was probably a wise choice.

TIME-HONORED TRUTH

One in the hand is worth two in the punsch.

Oogy wawa. (ANCIENT ZULU TOAST)

Horse's Neck with a Kick

1½ OUNCES WHISKEY
GINGER ALE
LEMON PEEL

Peel the lemon in a spiral, keeping the rind in one piece. Hook one end over the lip of a collins glass, allowing the rind to spiral to the bottom of the glass. Add ice cubes, pour in whiskey, and fill to the top with ginger ale.

HISTORICAL SURVEY

This drink originated in horse and buggy days when men were men and mares were nervous. It got its name because the rind of the lemon resembles the graceful neck of a thoroughbred as it arches to the bottom of the tumbler. The whiskey provides the kick.

TIME-HONORED TRUTH

Just remember, it's a very short journey from the horse's neck to the horse's ass.

Pithy Classical Allusion

The only unnatural sexual behavior is none at all. (SIGMUND FREUD)

Latin Manhattan

1½ OUNCES BACARDI AMBER

1 OUNCE SWEET VERMOUTH

1 OUNCE DRY VERMOUTH

2 DASHES BITTERS

Fill a cocktail shaker ¾ full of ice. Pour ingredients over ice and cover with top or bar glass. Shake with ice for five seconds and strain into a cocktail glass.

HISTORICAL SURVEY
Babbaloo!

TIME-HONORED TRUTH
To a cherry in rum, the world is rum.

There are more old drunkards than old physicians. (RABELAIS)

Blood and Sand

1   OUNCE SCOTCH

¾   OUNCE CHERRY BRANDY

¾   OUNCE SWEET VERMOUTH

¾   OUNCE ORANGE JUICE

Fill a cocktail shaker ¾ full of ice. Pour ingredients over ice and cover with top or bar glass. Shake with ice for five seconds and strain into a cocktail glass.

HISTORICAL SURVEY

This drink was given its name because of the brown and red colors of the liquors in the recipe. Legend also holds that this drink has been known to cause nosebleeds, which mixed with the sand on the floor at the desert-motif bar in which this cocktail was invented. See if this drink stands the test of time. Drink seven or eight and then blow your nose in the cat litter.

TIME-HONORED TRUTH

Real men don't say "Gesundheit."

Merry Widow

2   OUNCES DUBONNET
1½ OUNCES DRY VERMOUTH
**   LEMON TWIST**

Fill a cocktail shaker ¾ full of ice. Pour Dubonnet and vermouth over ice and cover with top or bar glass. Shake with ice for five seconds and strain into a cocktail glass. Garnish with a lemon twist.

HISTORICAL SURVEY

This drink was invented by a saucy seventeenth-century vixen. Amanda D'Amore was a celebrated micro-brewer (many women were, in Padua in those days), who is said to have sent her husband out to war in the hopes that he would be taken prisoner, which of course he was, being an incompetent warrior generally, and a real annoyance to his wily, hops-savvy wife. As the captors were familiar with the quality of Amanda's brew, the ransom they demanded was fourteen flagons of her best ale. When the kidnappers came to collect their ransom, she refused to pay, so they killed her husband. Amanda then invited the brigands in for a cold one and served them liberally on the house until they were too polluted to draw their firebrands, at which point she kidnapped the kidnappers and demanded a steep ransom of their wives (who weren't as clever as Amanda and paid the ransom), which included four hundred cases of Dubonnet, two hundred of vermouth, and twelve bushels of lemons. The widow combined these ingredients to make this cheerful potation, which kept her merry for many years to come.

Eat, drink, and be merry, for tomorrow your wife may ransom you for a case of rotgut and a coupl'a pounds of twists.

Down the Hatch

1 ½ OUNCES WHISKEY

3 DASHES BLACKBERRY BRANDY

2 DASHES BITTERS

ORANGE SLICE

Fill a cocktail shaker ¾ full of ice. Pour whiskey, brandy, and bitters over ice and cover with top or bar glass. Shake with ice for five seconds and strain into a cocktail glass. Garnish with orange.

HISTORICAL SURVEY

There is much speculation about what a hatch actually was historically, and what it must have been like to be down one. From what we have been able to piece together, however, it was a large trap door on a boat, covering the hold, which was a dark and dank place, probably containing rotting organic substances of one kind or another, producing a fermented and fruity atmosphere. It is no wonder that hatch dwellers eventually evolved a drink recipe such as this which invokes the fruity, fermented landscape of their subterranean world.

TIME-HONORED TRUTH

What goes down must come up.

Honolulu Lulu

- **1 OUNCE GIN**
- **1 OUNCE BENEDICTINE**
- **1 OUNCE MARASCHINO**

Fill a cocktail shaker ¾ full of ice. Pour ingredients over ice and cover with top or bar glass. Shake with ice for five seconds and strain into a cocktail glass.

HISTORICAL SURVEY
Aloha!

TIME-HONORED TRUTH
Oy!

Earthquake

1 OUNCE WHISKEY

1 OUNCE GIN

1 OUNCE PERNOD

Fill a cocktail shaker ¾ full of ice. Pour ingredients over ice and cover with top or bar glass. Shake with ice for five seconds and strain into a cocktail glass.

HISTORICAL SURVEY

When you drink this, the earth moves.

TIME-HONORED TRUTH

In the event of an earthquake, stay away from windows, live wires, and elevated freeways. If you can, find a door frame to cling to and stay there. You'll be less likely to spill your drink this way.

> Some weasel took the cork out of my lunch. (W. C. FIELDS)

Nightmare

1   OUNCE GIN

½   OUNCE DRY VERMOUTH

½   OUNCE CHERRY BRANDY

½   OUNCE ORANGE JUICE

Fill a cocktail shaker ¾ full of ice. Pour ingredients over ice and cover with top or bar glass. Shake with ice for five seconds and strain into a cocktail glass.

HISTORICAL SURVEY

Elkhalil Binebine, head archivist of the Queen's library and foremost proponent in his day of the controversial Dewey decimal system, is said to have turned in early one night after a dinner comprised of the inner organs of beasts and foul and a few too many pink gins. Obviously, he slept fitfully and had a bad dream in which his assistant, Clytemnestra, stood over him with a sword while he was in the bathtub and forced him to drink a martini with cherry brandy and orange juice. Although the thought harrowed him with fear and wonder the next morning, the Attic implications of his nightmare eventually got the better of him. He couldn't stop thinking about that drink and how it might taste, and how it might have transformed the course of Western history, and the Dewey decimal system, if Agamemnon had succumbed to Clytemnestra's demands and just taken his medicine. Maybe conciliation rather than war would have become the cornerstone of the Western tradition and powerful women would have been revered rather than villified. Unable to live with these questions any longer, he mixed a batch of the drink he had dubbed "the nightmare" and one night he and Clytemnestra sampled it. To their surprise, it tasted delicious, and the sword in the bathtub thing didn't work out too badly, either. So this story has a happy ending, although it is said that from this point forward, no one was able to find a single thing in the Queen's library stacks.

> "The cup of agony whereof I chant foams with a draught for thee." (AESCHYLUS, *THE ORESTEIA*)*
> *Dewey decimal call number A 10079.7645

Fallen Angel

- **2 OUNCES GIN**
- **2 DASHES WHITE CRÈME DE MENTHE**
- **1 DASH BITTERS**
- **JUICE OF 1 LEMON OR LIME**
- **CHERRY**

Fill a cocktail shaker ¾ full of ice. Pour gin, crème de menthe, bitters, and juice over ice and cover with top or bar glass. Shake with ice for five seconds and strain into a cocktail glass. Garnish with a cherry.

HISTORICAL SURVEY

It is believed that before the Fall, Satan stumbled into a dive bar called The Inferno and tasted this sinful concoction. After four or five, he uttered the immortal lines, "I'd rather reign in hell than serve in heaven," largely because he knew he couldn't order this drink in paradise (they only served frappés and soft drinks, and a little Mogen David on special occasions). Thus he traded eternity in paradise for a few hours of this earthly pleasure—and now you can, too.

TIME-HONORED TRUTH

Pride, gin, and white crème de menthe goeth before the Fall.

Five

Mellow
Jell-O Shots

From the beginning of time, gushy stuff has captured the imagination of men and women the world over, and the barroom is no exception. Since the invention of Jell-O some time in the 'thirties (back when the national mind-set was such that it would actually occur to someone to grind up a horse's hoof to make food congeal), people have been inventing bizarre things to do with it. The world of drinking and shots has proved a mother lode of squishy possibilities. Here's just a few.

Woo-Woo

¾ **CUP VODKA**
¼ **CUP PEACH SCHNAPPS**
1 **CUP WATER (HOT)**
1 **PACK CHERRY JELL-O**

Mix Jell-O and one cup hot water. Stir until Jell-O dissolves, add alcohol, pour into individual paper cups, and chill until firm.

An alcoholic is someone you don't like who drinks as much as you do. (DYLAN THOMAS)

Margarita

¾ **CUP TEQUILA**
¼ **CUP TRIPLE SEC**
1 **CUP WATER (HOT)**
1 **PACK LIME JELL-O**

Mix Jell-O and one cup hot water. Stir until Jell-O dissolves, add alcohol, pour into individual paper cups, and chill until firm.

Screwdriver

1   CUP VODKA

1   CUP WATER (HOT)

1   PACK ORANGE JELL-O

Mix Jell-O and one cup hot water. Stir until Jell-O dissolves, add alcohol, pour into individual paper cups, and chill until firm.

Melon Ball

¾   CUP VODKA

¼   CUP MIDORI MELON LIQUEUR

1   CUP WATER (HOT)

1   PACK ORANGE JELL-O

Mix Jell-O and one cup hot water. Stir until Jell-O dissolves, add alcohol, pour into individual paper cups, and chill until firm.

A friend told him that the particular drink he was drinking was slow poison, and he replied, "So who's in a hurry?"
—EXCERPT FROM ROBERT BENCHLEY, BY NATHANIEL BENCHLEY

Fuzzy Navel

- ¾ **CUP VODKA**
- ¼ **CUP PEACH SCHNAPPS**
- 1 **CUP WATER (HOT)**
- 1 **PACK ORANGE JELL-O**

Mix Jell-O and one cup hot water. Stir until Jell-O dissolves, add alcohol, pour into individual paper cups, and chill until firm.

I've been asked if I ever get the DT's. I don't know; it's hard to tell where Hollywood ends and the DT's begin. (W. C. FIELDS)

Daiquiri

- 1 **CUP RUM**
- 1 **CUP WATER (HOT)**
- 1 **CUP LIME JELL-O**

Mix Jell-O and one cup hot water. Stir until Jell-O dissolves, add alcohol, pour into individual paper cups, and chill until firm.

Watermelon

¾   CUP VODKA
¼   CUP MIDORI MELON LIQUEUR
1   CUP WATER (HOT)
1   PACK CHERRY JELL-O

Mix Jell-O and one cup hot water. Stir until Jell-O dissolves, add alcohol, pour into individual paper cups, and chill until firm.

> I drink to make other people interersting.
> (GEORGE JEAN NATHAN)

Lemon Drop

1   CUP VODKA
1   CUP WATER (HOT)
1   PACK LEMON JELL-O

Mix Jell-O and one cup hot water. Stir until Jell-O dissolves, add alcohol, pour into individual paper cups, and chill until firm.

> I always keep a supply of stimulant handy in case I see a snake—which I also keep handy.
> (W. C. FIELDS)

Kamikaze

¾ **CUP VODKA**

¼ **CUP TRIPLE SEC**

1 **CUP WATER (HOT)**

1 **CUP LIME JELL-O**

Mix Jell-O and one cup hot water. Stir until Jell-O dissolves, add alcohol, pour into individual paper cups, and chill until firm.

It's my number-one rule, and believe me I learned the hard way, when you're doing a Jell-O shot . . . don't inhale! (KIM, THE ACCIDENT-PRONE BARTENDER)

Vodka Gimlet

1 **CUP VODKA**
1 **CUP WATER (HOT)**
1 **PACK LIME JELL-O**

Mix Jell-O and one cup hot water. Stir until Jell-O dissolves, add alcohol, pour into individual paper cups, and chill until firm.

One final note on Jell-O shots. We've found that a little whipped cream on top of the Jell-O shots adds a little pizzazz . It should be mentioned, however, that exercising this option may also add a substantial cleaning fee to your bar bill.

Nonalcoholic Drinks

Yeah, right. . . . Get REAL.

There's Got to Be a Morning After—Surefire Hangover Remedies

No bar is complete without a few surefire, denial-inducing, medicinally moot miracle mixtures that cure nothing but your better instincts. Here's a few of our favorites.

Prairie Oyster

1½ OUNCES BRANDY

1 RAW EGG

1 DASH WORCESTERSHIRE SAUCE

SALT IF DESIRED

Carefully break the egg into a glass. Add Worcestershire sauce and brandy. Blend egg white and brandy gently, leaving yolk intact (that's the oyster part, and you wouldn't want to break the yolk and miss the awesome feeling you get when it slides whole down your throat). Of course, given the state of raw eggs these days, unless you are absolutely sure that your morning-after biochemistry is so toxic that it could kill anything, including salmonella, it may be wise to just chug the brandy and skip the rest.

My favorite hangover remedy is to shell an oyster, season to taste, then hawk it up your nose and out your mouth. Doesn't cure your hangover, but it sure takes your mind off your headache for a while. (KIM, THE ACCIDENT-PRONE BARTENDER)

Beer and Potato Salad

This is a favorite Midwestern remedy, where they'll use just about any excuse to consume massive quantities of both of these ingredients, so we can't vouch for it's effectiveness, but it is high on the comfort food scale.

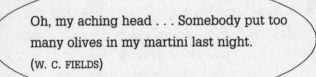

Oh, my aching head . . . Somebody put too many olives in my martini last night.
(W. C. FIELDS)

Bullshot

1½ OUNCES VODKA

3   OUNCES BEEF BOUILLON

1   SPLASH WORCESTERSHIRE SAUCE

SALT AND PEPPER TO TASTE

Fill a cocktail shaker ¾ full of ice. Pour ingredients over ice and cover with top or bar glass. Shake with ice for five seconds and strain into a cocktail glass.

Harry's Pick-Me-Up

2 OUNCES COGNAC
1 TEASPOON GRENADINE
JUICE OF ½ LEMON
CHAMPAGNE

Shake liquors over ice and strain into a champagne glass. Fill glass to the top with champagne. Be careful when you drink this as the bubbles have a tendency to creep up your nose, which can be really problematic during a formal brunch with a bunch of other hungover people who are trying their best to choke down eggs Florentine without rushing to call Ralph on the big white phone.

Morning Glory Fizz

1   OUNCE BITTERS
½ OUNCE PERNOD
1½ OUNCES WHISKEY
   WHITE OF 1 EGG
½ TEASPOON SUGAR
   JUICE OF ½ LIME
   SELTZER

Shake liquors, sugar, lime, egg, and bitters with ice and strain into a glass. Fill to the top with seltzer. This is a hangover remedy from a more puritanical time when people took a dash of penance with their hangover remedies. To make this remedy authentically, the hair of the dog should be the same brand as what bit you the night before. Doesn't quite have the same appeal first thing in the morning, does it? That single malt tastes just a little like swamp gas, doesn't it? Let that be a lesson to you.

NORA (reclining in bed with an ice bag):
What hit me?

NICK (with dry insouciance): The last martini.
—EXCERPT FROM THE THIN MAN,
BY DASHIELL HAMMETT

Beer Buster

1½ OUNCES 100-PROOF VODKA

CHILLED BEER OR ALE

2 DASHES TABASCO

Pour vodka into a collins glass filled with crushed ice.
Fill the remainder of the glass with beer, add Tabasco, and
stir lightly, then pound it. It is important to use crushed ice
to avoid the sound of the ice clanking against the glass as
you drink it. It's the small things that count first thing in the
morning.

Convivial Bartender Toasts

Here's to you and here's to me and may our friendship ever be, but
if perchance you don't agree, to hell with you and here's to me.
(A CHARMING TOAST FROM RICH, THE BOWLING ALLEY BARTENDER)

Engave

This is a Brazilian miracle drug that you can't buy in
this country, but we swear to God, it really works, even
though we have no idea how. Something about caffeine
and aspirin and rare zoological ions. The fact that you can't
buy it in this country is no doubt another vicious conspiracy on the part of the FDA to ensure that Americans pay
their dues for their partying. So, if you happen to be in Brazil
and come across this stuff, buy a few cases for us, will you?

Never mix, never worry. (MARTHA IN *WHO'S AFRAID OF
VIRGINIA WOOLF*, BY EDWARD ALBEE)

Bloody Caesar

½   **CUP BEER**

½   **CUP TOMATO JUICE**

Pour tomato juice into a glass and add beer. Think you can handle that?

Bloody Mary

1½   **OUNCES VODKA**

3   **OUNCES TOMATO JUICE**

2   **OUNCES BEEF BOUILLON**

    DASH TABASCO

    DASH HORSERADISH, SALT, PEPPER,

    CELERY SALT, GARLIC, LEMON, AND LIME

Mix it all together and you eat it all up.

Really Hot Menudo

They make this Mexican dish out of tripe. Just so you know, underneath all that hot pepper and broth is a steaming hunk of some cow's lower gastrointestinal tract.

Aspirin, Vitamins, and Three Glasses of Water the Night Before

Yeah, sure.

Twenty-four Hours

Besides abstinence, suffering through until the next day without utilizing a hair of the dog remedy is the only hangover cure guaranteed to work . . . every time.

Bon Mots from the Swingin' Set

I'd hate to be a teetotaler. Imagine getting up in the morning and knowing that's as good as you're going to feel all day. (DEAN MARTIN)

Eight

The Last Word in Good Taste— Tiny Tempters to Spread Your Reputation as a Knowing Host or Hostess

Tempting canapés are an important part of any social gathering. Whether or not you will be serving a meal as the main event, these delicious curtain raisers will spread your reputation as a host or hostess with the mostest, and it's so easy! Your spread of mouth-watering tidbits can be prepared ahead of time. Just do what Martha Stewart says and throw a hunk of wet Bounty over them until your guests arrive. Whatever the occasion, these little heart attacks on a plate will be sure to win finger-licking approval.

Bologna Boats

Place American cheese on slices of bologna and broil until the bologna curls. Serve with crackers.

Ham Rafts

Mix together ground boiled ham, grated cheddar and American cheeses, and condensed tomato soup. Season with horseradish, Worcestershire sauce, and mustard. Spread on toast squares and broil until browned.

Cheese Logs

1   **CUP PECANS**
1   **CLOVE GARLIC**
6   **OUNCES CREAM CHEESE**
1   **TABLESPOON STEAK SAUCE**
1½ **TABLESPOONS CHILI POWDER**
½ **TEASPOON CURRY**
½ **TEASPOON CUMIN**

Grind pecans and garlic. Blend with cream cheese and steak sauce. Shape into a log and roll in chili powder, curry, and cumin. Wrap in foil and chill until a firm log is formed. Serve with crackers.

Hothouse

Mix 8 ounces Limburger cheese with 2 tablespoons of butter. Add grated onion, garlic, salt, and pepper to taste. Serve with crackers.

Cheese Breeze

Mix cheddar cheese and crumbled, cooked bacon. Spread on toast and broil.

Salami Savories

Mix a can of condensed celery soup with 8 ounces cream cheese. Add ground salami, spread on toast, and broil.

Cheese Chips

Spread cheese over potato chips and broil. Serve promptly.

Cheese Franks

Spread cheese over franks and broil. Cut into bite-size hunks and serve promptly.

Sardine Snips

Mix chopped sardines with cream cheese. Spread on bread squares. Roll, fasten with party picks, and broil.

Tiny Broiled Sausages

Broil very small sausages.

Fish Bites with Chili Dip

16 OUNCES FROZEN FISH BITES
1   TABLESPOON CHILI SAUCE
1   DASH TABASCO
1   TABLESPOON STEAK SAUCE
1   CUP MAYONNAISE

Spread fish bites on greased baking sheet. Bake at 425 degrees for 10 minutes. Serve hot with chili dip made with the rest of the above ingredients.

Smoked Turkey Cigarettes

Spread cream cheese on smoked turkey slices, roll, and fasten with party picks.

Kipnips in Blankets

Select any of these kipnips. Wrap in thin strip of bacon, secure with party picks, and broil.

WATERMELON PICKLES
KIPPERED HERRING
STUFFED OLIVES
PICKLED ONIONS
SAUTÉED CHICKEN LIVERS

Bunch of Grapes

½ **POUND GRAPES**

Serves 6.

Tongue Treats

Combine ground, cooked tongue; chopped, cooked mushrooms; a chopped dill pickle; a splash of vermouth, and a large dollop of Thousand Island dressing. Spread on crackers.

Hot Ripe Olives

Drain can of ripe olives and heat them up.

Nine

Gay and Amusing Party Ideas

$\mathscr{T}$ired of the same old milling and swilling? With a little imagination, a few fake mustaches, and a lot of duct tape, you can treat your friends to a novel and exciting theme party evening that they'll be talking about for a long time to come. Here are a few unique ideas to set your mind to wandering.

Manic Monday Party

Start off your week with a Manic Monday bash. Your over-qualified, underpaid friends should excel at this theme party. Decor should include authority figures to burn in effigy and unemployment applications. For fun, invite your friends to wear their old name tags left over from jobs even worse than the ones they have now. Go around the table and relate amusing how-I-got-fired stories. Serve Blue Monday cocktails. Serve Ham Rafts and Bologna Boats to symbolize you sailing off into your own limited-future horizon.

Tank up Tuesday Party

Celebrate the execution-style slaying of another Monday with a Tank Up Tuesday party. Invoke an action adventure theme with drinks like Desert Storm or B-52's. Serve explosive appetizers like Hothouse treats, or Salami Savories. Be sure to have lots of matchbooks on hand for after-dinner special effects!

Historical Fun Fact

Early distillers would measure the proof of their whiskey by mixing it with gasoline and lighting it on fire. If it didn't blow up, it was too weak.

Wasted Wednesday Party

Ring in hump day with a romantic theme. Serve titillating, flirtatious drinks like Sex on the Beach, Foreplay, Slippery Nipple, or Come in a Hot Tub. For fun, turn out the lights and try to tell who is sitting next to you just by feeling them. Serve appetizers like a Bunch of Grapes and feed each other. One at a time, please! This is the nineties.

Thirsty Thursday Party

It's almost Friday. Turn up the heat, sweat like a pig, and drink like a fish.

Friday Fiesta

This Friday celebration has a south-of-the-border theme. Invite your guests to dress up as piñatas and then beat each other with sticks and see what pops out. Serve Latin Manhattans, or Trini Lopez Memorial Martinis. For fun, launch a coup d'état.

Saturday Morning Cartoon Club

Invite your guests to attend this celebration of your inner child in their pajamas. Watch cartoons with a pronounced sense of irony and make witty asides that demonstrate your cynical, postatomic perspective and underline the ultimate futility of all human endeavor. Serve whimsical kid's-stuff drinks like Dirty Girl Scout Cookies, Tootsie Rolls, Milkshakes or anything mixed with Hawaiian Punch. For fun, whine a lot.

Sinful Sunday

The only rule is, no virgins allowed.

Important Phone Numbers

POLICE

FIRE

DOCTOR

LIQUOR STORE

DRUG STORE

CLUB

ANALYST

NEIGHBORHOOD BAR

Favorite Drinks, Mine and My Friends'

_____

_____

_____

_____

_____

_____

_____

_____

_____

_____

_____

_____

_____

_____

_____

_____

Really Disgusting Drinks That I'll Never Drink Again Myself but May Consider Serving My Friends

_____

_____

_____

_____

_____

_____

_____

_____

_____

_____

_____

_____

_____

_____

_____

Audience Participation Page

If you have a favorite drink, send us your recipe and we'll put it in and credit you in the next edition of this book. We'll even include your legend and lore about the drink's origin. We do, however, reserve complete creative, aesthetic, and moral control regarding content and drinkability. We've spent a lot of time in bars, and we know what you guys are capable of.

Send recipes to the authors c/o:

The Berkley Publishing Group
200 Madison Avenue
New York, NY 10016

Absinthe Cocktail, 99
Alabama Slammer, 32
Amaratini, The, 84
Americano, The, 97
Au Currant, The, 89
B-52, 27
B.V.D.-tini, The, 68
Bar Slop, 43
Barking Dog, The, 67
Beanie Martini, The, 70
Beer Buster (hangover
    remedy), 129
Bees' Knees, The, 100
Between the Sheets, 101
Blood and Sand, 109
Bloody Caesar (hangover
    remedy), 130
Bloody Mary (hangover
    remedy), 130
Blow Job, 10
Blue Monday, 96
Blue Sapphire, 66
Brain Hemorrhage, The, 15
Brainstorm, The, 103
Bronx Zoo, The, 69
Bullshot (hangover remedy),
    126
Cajun Martini, The, 72
Cement Mixer, 16
Chocolate Martini, The, 86
Classic Martini, The, 52
Come in a Hot Tub, 47
Cosmopolitan, 55
Crest Shot, The, 46
Dentyne, 20
Depth Charge, 26

Desert Storm, 21
Dirty Girl Scout Cookie, 18
Down the Hatch, 111
Drunk Monk, The, 87
Earthquake, 113
Eclipse The, 61
Engave (hangover remedy),
    129
Fallen Angel, 115
Fibber Magee, 60
Flaming Dr Pepper, 19
Flaming Lemon Drop, 41
Florentine Martini, 80
Flu, The, 102
Foreplay, 13
Gamekeeper's Martini, The,
    64
Greta Garbo Cocktail, 106
Gunga Din, 74
Harry's Pick-Me-Up
    (hangover remedy), 127
Honolulu Lulu, 112
Horse's Neck with a Kick, 107
James Bond Martini, The, 56
Jell-O Shots,
    Daiquiri, 119
    Fuzzy Navel, 119
    Kamikaze, 121
    Lemon Drop, 120
    Margarita, 117
    Melon Ball, 118
    Screwdriver, 118
    Vodka Gimlet, 122
    Watermelon, 120
    Woo-Woo, 117
Kamikaze, 30

Kangaroo, The, 98
Kir Martini, 78
Knockout, The, 75
Latin Manhattan, 108
Liquid Heroin, 29
Mango, 35
Melon Ball, 36
Melontini, The, 84
Mentos Popper, 44
Merry Widow, 110
Mikey Special, The, 45
Milk Shake, 48
Mind Eraser, 14
Morning Glory Fizz (hangover
   remedy), 128
Mud Slide, 22
Naked Aviator, 12
Negroni, 76
Nightmare, 114
Orgasm, 34
Pansy, The, 104
Pineapple Bomber, 40
Prairie Fire, 24
Prairie Martini, The, 62

Prairie Oyster (hangover
   remedy), 125
Quickie, 95
Really Hot Menudo (hangover
   remedy), 130
Red Death, 33
Rhett Butler, 94
Russian Martini, The, 90
Russian Quaalude, 37
Scarlett O'Hara, 93
Sex on the Beach, 6
Slippery Nipple, 8
Snake Bite, 25
Spitball, The, 42
Sunset Martini, 58
Tequila Popper, 38
TNT-ini, The, 59
Tootsie Roll, 11
Trini Lopez Memorial Martini,
   The, 88
Volga Boatman, The, 82
Watermelon Shot, 31
Weep No More, 105
Woo-Woo, 28